MW00620545

LIVING
UP TO
DEATH

PAUL RICOEUR

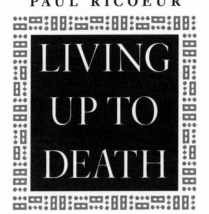

LIVING
UP TO
DEATH

TRANSLATED BY DAVID PELLAUER

THE UNIVERSITY OF CHICAGO PRESS
CHICAGO & LONDON

PAUL RICOEUR (1913–2005) was one of the leading French philosophers of
the twentieth century and the John Nuveen Professor in the Divinity School,
the Department of Philosophy, and the Committee on Social Thought of
the University of Chicago. In 2000 he was awarded the Kyoto Prize by the
Inamori Foundation and in 2004 the Kluge Prize by the Library
of Congress for lifetime achievement.

DAVID PELLAUER is professor of philosophy at DePaul University.

Originally published as *Vivant jusqu'à la mort suivi de Fragments* copyright © Éditions du Seuil 2007.

The University of Chicago Press, Chicago 60637
The University of Chicago Press, Ltd., London
© 2009 by The University of Chicago
All rights reserved. Published 2009
Printed in the United States of America
18 17 16 15 14 13 12 11 10 09   1 2 3 4 5

ISBN-13: 978-0-226-71349-6 (cloth)
ISBN-10: 0-226-71349-0 (cloth)

LIBRARY OF CONGRESS CATALOGING-IN-PUBLICATION DATA
Ricoeur, Paul.
  [*Vivant jusqu'à la mort.* English]
  Living up to death / Paul Ricoeur ; translated by David Pellauer.
    p. cm.
  Includes bibliographical references.
  ISBN-13: 978-0-226-71349-6 (cloth : alk. paper)
  ISBN-10: 0-226-71349-0 (cloth : alk. paper) 1. Death.
  2. Death—Religious aspects—Christianity. 3. Philosophy,
  Modern—20th century. 4. Philosophy, French—20th century.
  5. Christianity—Meditations. 6. Ricoeur, Paul. I. Title.
  B2430.R553V5813 2009
  236'.1—dc22

                                        2008026873

♾ The paper used in this publication meets the minimum requirements of
the American National Standard for Information Sciences—Permanence
of Paper for Printed Library Materials, ANSI Z39.48-1992.

CONTENTS

PREFACE

Paul Ricoeur continued to think about the separation between the time of writing, which belongs to the mortal time of an individual life, and the time of publication, which opens the time of every work to a "durability unaware of death." In this sense, any author is, sadly, so to speak, obligated to withdraw, as Ricoeur writes in his fragment on Watteau, into the limited frame of mortal time, while his writing, his thoughts, can step beyond this frame and reinscribe themselves in the transhistorical time "of the reception of this work by other living beings who have their own time."

It is as if, then, something is thereby completed. It is as if this closure of a work is the condition for its being open to interpretation, as Ricoeur said in many of his works, so that it is cast free from the author's intentions and its initial context. Yet the fragments offered here to such a reading do retain a touch of incompleteness. They are in most instances sketches, rough first drafts, unorganized notes that he would probably have set aside once he had returned to them and reworked them, something that did not happen. We should not overestimate their importance. Yet, how are we to preserve, among the papers now in the Ricoeur Archive,[1] such fragments through which one can experience so well Ricoeur's moves, his style, his way of thinking, his life even, here left incomplete because death cut it off? There is surely a way here to see a thought at work, almost in action, with everything about it that is fleeting, vulnerable, ephemeral—and also a precious testimony, intentionally left behind by their author.

In offering a few prefatory comments, I would like simply to indicate a few of the main lines to be found in Ricoeur's meditating about death, drawing on the three questions he announced in the winter of 1995–1996 as setting his program, ones that seem to run through these fragments from one end to the other: 1) "imagined figures" (what representation can I give myself?); 2) "mourning and cheerfulness" (what is their root?); and 3) "Am I still a Christian?" (along with In what way am I not a "Christian philosopher"?). To these questions I would add what he has to say about the meaning of the resurrection, which recurs at several points, as if it were a matter of a too radical representation, a too noniconic one, beyond any figure or image, to be eliminated. I will not address these questions as a specialist in philosophy, for I do not see myself in that role. I want instead to consider them in terms of something like an interrupted conversation between friends, one of his many such conversations. If I could keep just one thing from what my friend said, it would be what he said to me one time when I was feeling somewhat dejected: "Get on with life." He meant by this that there are two difficult choices to accept in life, to really accepting life. The first is that one is mortal; the second is that one cannot be loved by everyone.

FOREGOING REPRESENTATIONS

To make sense of what Ricoeur was trying to do we have to begin soberly. We might even say we must begin by adopting the same ascetic attitude toward our own imagination as the one through which he approaches these questions. For Ricoeur begins by clearing away the undergrowth of what has been imagined in order to analyze our representations regarding death critically. In these thoughts about mourning, which in some ways are preliminary sketches of the much more fully developed pages in *Memory, History, Forgetting*, he first takes up the impossibility of imagining what or where those closest to us who have died now are.[2] Next, he turns to the impossibility of imagining ourselves dead, or even as dying. Finally, there is the unclear case of the indistinct mass of the dead struck down by something like the spread of a contagious deadly disease. Through this kind of clarification, along with the work of memory that heals a misleading imagination, our flood of images is confined to its banks and not allowed to overflow. Attaining this ascetic attitude thus requires a conceptual clarification that itself has a cathartic value, and it is through such a clarification that his text on mourning begins. In the same way, at the close, it is through an analysis of the meanings of the word "resurrection" that the fragments end.

There is something agnostic—in the proper and strict sense of a philosophical critique that does not allow itself to be led astray, that prefers to focus on the aporia, the puzzle that holds up thinking—about this refusal to imagine, to "represent" another side, to objectify another world. It is the end [*fin*] contained in the meaning of "finitude," which turns us back to this side, to the world in which we live, the only world we have.[3] And is not perhaps such a puzzle about resurrection required to open the possibility of thinking through a poetics? Yet this agnosticism is not incompatible with the terseness of the gospel. For "we do not know," and Calvin himself, who in refusing any cult of the dead asked to be buried like the poor in a common grave, had affirmed that we must first of all rid ourselves of all concern for our own salvation. But we must be careful. It is not a question here of some kind of Stoic asceticism that would be a way of preparing for death, a way of anticipating oneself as already a corpse. On the contrary, from his early philosophy of the will on, Ricoeur fought against this kind of impossible anticipation, which he criticized in Heidegger.[4]

It is here that the foregoing of representations reveals a fundamental moment in the work of mourning and the accepted finitude of having been born and of being mortal, in that dialectic of refusal and consent that Ricoeur had earlier so superbly explored.[5] How can one ever stop pulling oneself together, seeking "who" one is, mobilizing one's forces, one's memories, one's desire, in what he called the "insouciance" of an appetite for life, which is sometimes a struggle, agony, but for all that one of the deepest forms of that insouciance he calls "cheerfulness"? How at the same time does one consent to leave one's place to another self, one whom I do not know, to others, how does one consent to effacing oneself before all others, in that insouciance, that letting go of oneself, which would be the other essential form of cheerfulness? Is there not a narrow path between the excessive concern for the self of Stoicism and the excessive unconcern of Orphism, where this road has to lead in the "end"? The limit in this sense reveals an oscillation internal to our most ordinary forms of existence. And hope transforms itself into that low-key, almost Franciscan fraternity of "being among" creatures, yet without renouncing being oneself, to the end, of taking one's place at the very moment one yields it.

AN ESSENTIAL CHEERFULNESS

This is why we cannot separate cheerfulness from mourning: "Only those who mourn will be comforted," Ricoeur writes in his notes for the plan for his manuscript presented below. This is perhaps one of the places where he was close to Derrida. Melancholy is not something that we must avoid at all costs, for it is a part of our condition, such that our reality, to be alive, must also include the absence of what no longer is but once was. This reality cannot be absorbed by either a death that would be more real than any life or by the illusion that life alone is real and that death always dissolves it.[6] Yet the mourning we must undergo for those dear to us but absent returns in our anticipation of the mourning others close to us will have to undergo when we shall have disappeared (see *Memory, History, Forgetting*, 360). This first doubling prepares the way for a second one, which is really what is essential, what he calls the "relation of our desire to live" in relation to all others. I shall come to this.

However the model for this redoubling is already situated in the more primary turning from death back toward birth, a turn Ricoeur took up in the 1950s in his philosophy of the will, and that he continued to pursue over the course of *Memory, History, Forgetting*. Mourning representation points to the impossible experience of one's own death as well as of one's own birth—which has either not happened yet or always already has happened, making existence a stretch of time where birth always has an irreversible priority. As he says, with Hannah Arendt, men "are not born to die but in order to begin" (*Memory, History, Forgetting*, 489).

There is therefore an intimate bond between mourning and cheerfulness, between lamentation and praise. Just as mourning oscillates between refusal and consent, cheerfulness oscillates between struggle or the appetite for life and the grace of insouciance. Beyond this explanatory moment, from a practical point of view, we find a profound analogy between the plaintive cry of suffering at the end of his little essay on evil and the hymn that sings of gratitude at the end of *The Course of Recognition*.[7] In both cases—and this is essential if we are to understand Ricoeur's refusal of any idea of a last judgment—it is a matter of getting beyond all thought of retribution, reward, or punishment. It is a question of grace, of the absurd in its purest form, of unhappiness as well as happiness—even if this "Buddhist moment" still has something of a Protestant air to it, or one linked to reading Job.

Be that as it may, we are now close to what is essential, to that experience of the pure goodness of existing, as though the proximity of death were to fracture every confessional limitation, releasing the languages in which our deepest experiences have been held. Here the resources of life outrun individual concerns and open us through compassion to the desire for existence of every other existing being. At the same time, however, the one who dies always dies alone, even when he does not do so alone but accompanied to the end by the fraternal proximity of those who then are the ones really closest to him.

THE MEANING OF RESURRECTION

This foregoing of representation, or of the presence of something absent, turns out to be the condition for an experience essential to living well, whether this takes the form of a lively desire to exist that vehemently runs counter to every threat to life, or is one of detachment and unconcern for oneself yet one filled with gratitude. Here it is worth noting how the final text in the little fragment presented here, in *On Mourning and Cheerfulness*, and titled "Death," takes us in two directions. We now have two ways of speaking of what is essential, that of self-detachment, which prepares for the transfer of one's love of life to others, and that of confidence in God's care, which takes up, elevates, and supports my insouciance. This confidence in a resurrection that we cannot imagine is explored in terms of several different figures, including that of abandoning oneself to God's memory, where each existence makes a difference. This idea, which Ricoeur borrows from Whitehead, seems to him a way of schematizing in the form of "process" an eternal present for which we have no image. Here we shift from an agnostic sense of resurrection to its poetic expression.

In *Critique and Conviction* Ricoeur had distinguished between a horizontal resurrection, which passes through others, through the transmission, reception, and the taking up of my words, acts, and thoughts into those of others, and a vertical resurrection, into the memory of a God powerful enough to recapitulate everything, into this God's "today." At the end of his fragments Ricoeur courageously starts over again, and distinguishes among the senses of resurrection as a narrative proof and the fulfilling of a promise, as a spring-like experience of a return to life against death, and as the eschatological limit and hope regarding what is not yet.

I hope the reader will allow me to recall a personal memory here. Toward the end of 1995, Paul asked me to undertake a correspondence with him about death and life, including all these questions. In January 1996, I sent him a twenty-page letter expanding on his "admissions without being confessions" in *Critique and Conviction*, where he had placed his meditation on "the rigor required by the renunciation of the idea of afterlife, under the twofold sign of Eckhartian 'detachment' and of Freudian 'work of mourning.' To use a language that remains quite mythical, I would say this: Let God, at my death, do with me as he wills. I demand nothing, I demand no 'after.' I cast upon others, my survivors, the task of taking up again my desire to be, my effort to exist, in the time of the living."[8]

At that moment, our conversation was not about resurrection, for I fully shared his refusal to seek in it a form of afterlife.[9] But I wrote to him about my distrust of this idea of a huge memory of God where the least things would be preserved without loss. I saw in this something like a giant monad capable of comprehending, of justifying everything. Smiling he said to me, "you mean I have to give up even that?" So I yielded while protesting, and proposed looking for a handhold in the plurality of forms of memory.

In April 1999 we were able to continue this conversation during a twelve-day trip the two of us took to Cappadocia in Turkey. He was doing the final editing on his magnificent "three-masted" *Memory, History, Forgetting*, and navigating, by way of the melancholy of history, toward an almost Bergsonian philosophy of life, like a river headed toward its estuary. Therefore, the central topic of our conversation was largely about Life, a theme I feared might fudge the issue by wiping out all individual differences. And so, even while admiring his courage in continually opting for the desire for life, I recalled to him that in the most radical texts of the Christian tradition resurrection was not an ongoing continuation of life by way of the immortality of the soul, but something that responded from above to the real discontinuity of birth and death, and that touched the singularity of living bodies, those irreplaceable existences that remain at the end of life's road and that disappear there never to return again.[10]

"I AM NOT A CHRISTIAN PHILOSOPHER"

This was the very question Ricoeur posed to himself, that of an "infinitely more radical salvation than the justification of sinners: the justification of existence." And this is what seemed to him to be at the base of Jesus's own attitude in the face of death. For Jesus, if we follow the suggestion of Xavier Léon Dufour, did not think in terms of some distant future, but, by means of a demythologization of judgment and even of pardon, of a different kind of present—one expanded to include the still-there of what had been and the already-here of what might be. This is the proximity of the Kingdom, in the lilies of the field and the birds of the air, about which Ricoeur said, citing Kierkegaard, at the end of *Memory, History, Forgetting*, that they do not labor. But this thought needs to be set alongside the question indicated in the plan he outlined in the text presented here: "Am I still Christian?" This is a discreet, unexpected question,[11] but one that throws a cloud over the final fragments as a whole.

It may be helpful to point to some things in the texts brought together here that shake up not only the prejudice against Ricoeur as a "Christian philosopher," but also against the indulgent and telltale image of him as a resolute Christian to the end. There was something like a radical doubt in him, which gives credibility to his own testimony. To be sure, he spoke of his faith as something he was born to, and hence something both relative and accepted: "chance transformed into destiny by a continuous choice."[12] But already here we can see him taking some distance on the notion of *pistis*, of faith understood as absolute adhesion.[13] Moreover, if the problem is not resurrection as an answer to death by announcing a still more singular form of life after death, nor that of the grace that responds to sin by announcing the abolition of every debt through a first, unmerited gift, what is preaching to say today—in reply to what question? That of existence as absurd? But in what way?

Or, to take up the question in the opposite way: what is the actual "call" to which philosophical understanding has to reply responsibly? And what are we to make of the biblical saga as a whole, which unlike the *Odyssey* presents itself as a true "history," when it turns out to be in large part a theological-political fiction? In the end, what tormented Ricoeur in his relation to the figure of Jesus was the impossible alternative of seeing in him only an ethical teacher, even an exceptional one, as in some liberal forms of Protestantism, or, on the contrary, of seeing in him the sacrificial figure of the very Son of God the Father, dying in our place. What can it mean that he died "for us"? Must we resign ourselves to the bland moralism of a humanity finally having reached its majority, but having nonetheless lost the moral vehemence of the desire for life that would be a giving of oneself with no expectation of a return, a giving that goes beyond morality—or of the reception of oneself by another? Or must we, on the contrary, just resolve ourselves to cling blindly to a sacrificial theology that presupposes a vindictive, judgmental God, one captive to his threats, promises, and punishments?[14]

What is certain, in any case, is that Ricoeur refused the title "Christian philosopher." A philosopher is a philosopher through and through, allowing nothing to impede his questioning, since anything that impedes it also arouses it. A philosopher is also someone aware of the contingency of having been born into a language, as well as of the plurality of human phenomena. And he accepts being confronted by controversy, by something that brings together the irreducible dissymmetry and reciprocity of points of view. Ricoeur even speaks of the autarchy and "self-sufficiency" of philosophical inquiry, no doubt an ex-

cessive expression, unrepresentative of his own concrete practice as a philosopher, always in dialogue
with his sources and other disciplines, but one that
does speak, in its place, of the almost Nietzschean vehemence of his philosophical self-affirmation. Which
is to say, it is with what he is, with his mind, his concern for making sense, his passion for argument, that
the philosopher "responds" (in a responsible manner)
to the properly religious call which speaks of the first,
sudden appearance of things, of the pleasure of existing, of anonymous devotion, and of overturning the
world.

What also stands out forcefully from this essay
and these fragments, some parts now more than a doz-
en years old, is the reversal by which the concern for
oneself is redirected toward others. Not as a sacrifice,
but as a gift that forgets itself, as incognito service,[15]
where the neighbor is simply someone who acts as a
neighbor—for the theme of the neighbor determines
a radical reversal: a redoubling of concern detached
from oneself so as to relate it to others. This may be
the claim of a resurrection for others that I do not ask
for myself. It may be, as we see in the fragment on
Derrida, the confident handing over to others of the
traces that I leave, which ask to be recalled, reopened,
rethought. It may even be the transfer to others of my

desire to live, in its invulnerability, its being stronger than death. It may be here that we find what is Christian about what Paul Ricoeur the philosopher has to say, similar in this way to the Christian expression of a picture by Rembrandt or the musical one of a piece by Bach.[16] The question then is no longer one of an infinite grieving for someone who, as all too often in human history, died for no reason, but rather one of infinite recognition as regards someone who was not born for nothing—and this perhaps should be said of everyone.

Olivier Abel

EDITORS' NOTE

The text that follows scrupulously respects Paul Ricoeur's manuscript, which was transcribed by Catherine Goldenstein, who spells out in her postface the circumstances and moment when these pages were written.

Not having intended to publish a facsimile of the manuscript, we have not reproduced line for line the layout of the text, which is simply contingent, except for the opening page, which presents the plan for the first part of the proposed book, and for the last page, which ends the second part and speaks of the end of the book. However, we have preserved the breaks between paragraphs. And we have corrected or introduced punctuation marks where these were missing or erroneous, as well as correcting a few obvious mistakes in writing, in order to respect current conventions regarding typography when publishing a book. For example, where Ricoeur underlined words they are here italicized.

Notes regarding the manuscript are given in

square brackets in bold; for example, regarding paragraphs that were crossed out or added in the margin, or for words that were difficult or impossible to decipher and could only be guessed at, or where they were simply missing. We have not attempted to indicate or reproduce minor erasures. Further information is also given in notes about the authors and titles that Ricoeur alludes to or the passages cited. A few notes are Ricoeur's own and are indicated as such.

Catherine Goldenstein and Jean-Louis Schlegel

UP
TO
DEATH

MOURNING

&

CHEERFULNESS

Jusqu'à la mort : du deuil et de la gaîté.

—

Par où commencer ce tardif apprentissage ? Par l'essentiel,
tout de suite ? Par la nécessité et la difficulté de faire le
deuil de sa vie ─ vouloir ─ exister après la mort ? de la joie ─ non,
plutôt la gaîté jointe à la grâce enfantine existe-t-il vivant jusqu'à la mort ?

Non : l'essentiel est trop proche, donc trop recouvert,
trop dissimulé. Il se découvrira peu à peu, à la fin.

Je commencerai par le plus abstrait en ce sens le plus
ainsi à dire, à particulier.

Non par
l'imaginaire
qui recouvre
et dissimule.

Le plus abstrait ? les équivoques de la mort, du mot mort.

Je vois trois significations majeures — peut-être plus ? — qu'il
importe de distinguer ; car c'est leur empiètement mutuel
et la confusion qui en résulte qui entretiennent l'amorçage
épaisse de la mort. À cet égard, je le pense ici comme
face à d'autres situations la confusion conceptuelle, la clarification
conceptuelle a déjà valeur thérapeutique. C'est là la tâche
minimale de la réflexion philosophique : analyser, clarifier.

① → Il y a d'abord la rencontre de la mort d'un autre chose,
des autres inconnus. Quelqu'un a disparu. Une question surgit
obstinément : existe-t-il encore ? et où ? en quel ailleurs ?
sous quelle forme invisible à nos yeux ? visible autrement ?
Cette question, lie la mort au mort, aux morts. C'est une question
de vivants, de bien portants dirigée plus loin la question
d'êtres sont les morts ? si insistante que même
dans nos sociétés sécularisés vous ne savez pas quoi faire des
morts, c'est-à-dire des cadavres. Nous ne les jetons pas aux
ordures comme des déchets domestiques que physiquement ils
sont pourtant. Et c'est pourtant cette question que je veux
exorciser, dont je veux faire le deuil pour moi-même. Pourquoi ?

Pourquoi ?

Parce que mon rapport à la mort non encore échue est

UP TO DEATH

MOURNING AND CHEERFULNESS

1. The figures of the imaginary

2. Mourning and Cheerfulness

3. Am I still a Christian

Notes

Lamenting and mourning

Isaiah 40

Consolation and mourning

Contestation and mourning: the peak of lamenting

Who am I that . . .

I am nothing . . .

Dry grass. from Isaiah 40:7–8

Note: This text was found in a file folder marked with the title "Until Death, Mourning and Cheerfulness. P.R." It was undoubtedly begun sometime around 1996. Also included in this folder were two letters, dated 20/1/96 and April '96, along with the readings for the Sunday worship service of 28 May 1995.

Reprise of the "sorrow of finitude" (Vol. and Invol.)[1]

Mourning and Consent → joy/cheerfulness

    Hope   —transgenerational

            —cosmopolitical

            —ecclesial; the cloud of witnesses

    The living and the dead? No, the living and the memory of the dead in the memory of the living. Bond of memory

    What is man that you should remember him!

    Only those who mourn shall be comforted

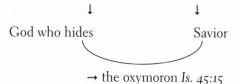

    → the oxymoron *Is.* 45:15

    "Truly, you are a God *who hides himself,* O God of Israel, the *Savior*"

    → (hidden—savior)

Follow the thread "do not fear"

    From the word addressed to the king

    before battle

(O.T. Th. Römer)[2] through the N.T.

    until "consolation" (in the sense of Isaiah 40f.) before the agony

    The agonistic *until* . . .

Take up again the tradition of *lamentation* and *wailing*

    in Psalms, Jeremiah, Isaiah III

Must let the lament *speak* as the ultimate vis-à-vis of mourning.

    Mourning passing through the lament → (do its) mourning *of* the lament

    The Buddhist moment? End of the book of Job; I place my hand over my mouth . . .

[THIS IS FOLLOWED BY PAGES OF THE HANDWRITTEN MANUSCRIPT NUMBERED 1–16. THEY CORRESPOND TO POINT 1 ABOVE.]

UP TO DEATH

MOURNING AND CHEERFULNESS

Where to begin this late apprenticeship? By what is essential, right away? by the necessity and difficulty of mourning a wanting-to-exist after death? by joy— no, instead, with cheerfulness joined to a hoped-for grace of existing until death?

No: the essential is too close, therefore too covered over, too hidden. It will reveal itself bit by bit, at the end.

[THE FOLLOWING THREE PARAGRAPHS ARE CROSSED OUT IN ORDER TO BE MOVED BELOW. WE REPRODUCE THEM HERE SINCE THERE IS NO LATER PLACE IN WHICH TO INSERT THEM.]

I will begin with what is most abstract, in this sense, easiest to speak of, to articulate. [IN THE MARGIN NEXT TO THIS SENTENCE THERE IS A CORRECTION: No, by the make-believe that covers it over— and hides it.]

The most abstract? The equivocations of death, of the word death.

I see three major meanings—maybe more?—that need to be distinguished, for it is their mutual overlapping and the confusion that results from this that leads to the foreboding anxiety about death. In this regard, here I think of things like when faced with other situations of conceptual confusion, conceptual clarification already has a therapeutic value. Here, as elsewhere, this is the minimal task for philosophical reflection: analyze, clarify. [END OF THE PARAGRAPHS CROSSED OUT.]

1. There is first of all the encounter with the death of a loved other, of unknown others. Someone has disappeared. One question comes up obstinately again and again: does he still exist? and where? where else? in what form invisible to our eyes? visible in another way? This question connects death with the dead person, the dead ones. It is a question for the living, perhaps for those in good health I shall say later. The question What sort of beings are the dead? is so insistent that even in our secularized societies we do not know what to do with the dead, that is, with the cadavers. We don't throw them in the garbage like domestic waste, which they physically are, however. The make-believe proceeds by a slide and generalization: my death, our deaths, the dead. Generalization

by dissipating the differences: the loved one → the third person. The dead like disappeared third persons, the deceased, the day of the Dead. The place of sepulture, among the criteria of humanity, along with tools, language, moral and social norms, the testimony of antiquity and the persistence of this certain fact [?]: one does not get rid of the dead, one is never finished with them.

And yet it is this kind of questioning about the lot of the dead that I want to exorcise, for which I want to do the mourning for myself. Why?

Why?

Because my own relation to a death which hasn't yet happened is obscured, obliterated, altered by the anticipation and internalization of the question about the lot of the already dead dead. It is tomorrow's death, in the future perfect tense, so to speak, that I imagine. And it is this image of the dead person I will be for others that takes up all the room, with its load of questions: what are, where are, how are the dead?

My struggle is with and against this *image* of tomorrow's dead, this dead person that I shall be for the survivors. With and against that *make-believe* where death is in some way sucked up by the dead person and all the dead. To begin the struggle against this make-believe, I will take up again the analysis at the point where I introduced the reference to survivors. The first fact is this one. Others still alive survive the death of their own. In the same way, others will survive me. The question of survival is thus first of all a question about the survivors who ask themselves whether the dead do continue to exist, in the same chronological time or at least in a temporal register parallel to that of the living, even if this mode of time is held to be imperceptible. All the answers given by cultures concerning the survival of the dead are connected to this question not called into question: passage to another state, expectation of resurrection, reincarnation, or, for more philosophical minds, change of temporal status, elevation to an immortal eternity. But these answers are to a question posed by the survivors, concerning the lot of the already dead dead.

I come back to the key word in my answer about why the mourning I want to enter into—as a work of mourning . . . : the internalization before my death of a question *post mortem*, of the question: what are the dead? To see myself dead before being dead, and to apply to myself in anticipation a survivor's question. In short, the dread of the future perfect. I said, in passing, that it is a question for those in good health. In effect, its capacity to give rise to dread is strongest when it comes to disturb, confront, insult the insolence of our appetite for an invulnerable life. This adjective "invulnerable" brings into play the difference from what I shall say below, later, toward the end, if my discourse gets there, the joy of living to the end, hence about the appetite for a life colored by a certain insouciance that I call cheerfulness. But let's not go too fast. We aren't there yet. We are only at the beginning. That is, with abstractions, mixed-up meanings, confusions that need to be *clarified*.

[THE FOLLOWING PARAGRAPH HAS A NOTE IN THE MARGIN: in its place? No.]

The third idea about death is mortality, obliged-to-die one day, having to die. Philosophies of finitude have undertaken to make this category of existence the high point of their reflection. In this way, they make it a corollary, a variant of finitude. They carry to the extreme their proposal when they think of finitude, of being toward the end or for the end, from within, I mean with a gaze that forbids itself a bird's-eye view, one from above, on a boundary whose two sides could be looked at—from above. Seen from within, finitude goes toward a limit beginning from the inside and not toward a boundary that our gaze can cross, leading to the question: *quid* afterward? In

a sense, my meditation is akin to that of these think-
ers about finitude. But, contrary to appearances, finitude is an abstract idea. The idea that I must die one
day, I do not know when, or how, carries too flimsy a
certitude (*mors certa, hora incerta*) for my desire to
take hold of—what I shall call below (distinguishing
the two phrases): a desire to be, an effort to exist. I
am well aware of everything that has been written
and said about anxiety about one day no longer existing. But, if the path has to be taken up again of an accepted finitude, it is after the struggle with the make-
believe death concerning which I have so far spoken
of only one of its figures, the internalized anticipation of a death tomorrow for which I will be dead for
the survivors, for my survivors.

2. [IN THE MARGIN BEFORE THE NUMBER 2: about the
figures of the make-believe] A second meaning is attached to the word death. Dying as an event: passing,
ending, finishing. In one way, my dying tomorrow is
on the same side as my being-already-dead tomorrow.
On the side of the future perfect tense. What we call
a dying person is one only for those who attend his
agony, who maybe help him in his agony—I shall return to this below. To think of myself as one of these
dying people is to imagine myself as the dying person

I shall be for those who attend my dying. Nevertheless the difference between these two make-believe situations is large. To be present at a death is more precise, more poignant that simply surviving. Taking part is a more point-like test, more event-like. To survive is a long trajectory, at best that of mourning, that is, of the accepted separation from the dead person who takes a distance on, becomes detached from the living so that he can survive. But, in the end, it is still for me an internalized anticipation, the most terrifying one, that of the dying person I shall be for those who attend my death. Well! I am saying that it is the anticipation of this agony that constitutes the concrete core of the "fear of death," among all the confused meanings that overlap one another.

This is why I want first to confront this idea of death as an anticipated agony. To do this, I shall force myself to free the inevitable anticipation of dying and of its agony from the image of the dying person looked at by the other. Help will come first from the testimony of physicians "specialized(?)" in the palliative care given those with AIDS, incurable cancer, in short, those in the terminal phase of their illness. They do not say that it is easy to die. They do say two or three things that are important to me. First, this: so long as they remain lucid ill dying people do not see themselves as dying, as soon to be dead, but as still living, and this can be, I have learned from Mme Hacpille, even up to a half hour before their dying. Still living, this is the important word. Next, again this: what occupies one's still preserved thoughts is not concern for what there is after death, but rather the mobilization of the deepest resources of life to still affirm itself. The deepest resources of life: what does that say? Here I am anticipating. I cannot not anticipate. For it is this experience that is going to help me separate the anticipation of agony from the anticipation in the gaze of an external spectator distinct from the dying person. The ground of the ground of the testimony of the physician from the palliative care unit is that the internal grace that distinguishes the dying person consists in the emergence of the *Essential* within the very framework of the time of agony. This vocabulary of the Essential will accompany me throughout this meditation. I anticipate, I am anticipating again: the Essential, in one sense (what I will try to say below with greater exactitude) is the religious; it is, if I dare put it this way, that which is common to every religion and what, at the threshold of death, transgresses the consubstantial limitations of confessing and confessed religions. I have said it often enough, I do not scorn what I call, to put it quickly, "codes" (I have in

mind Blake's *Great Code* as used by Northrop Frye);[3]
no, but the religious is like a fundamental language
that exists only in natural, historically limited languages. Just as everyone is born into *a* language and
accedes to other languages only by a second apprenticeship, and most often, only through translation,
the religious exists culturally only as articulated in
the language and code of a historical religion; language and code articulate only on the condition of
filtering, and in this sense limiting that amplitude,
that depth, that density of the religious that I am here
calling the Essential. Having said this, what the physician in the palliative care unit bears witness to is the
grace granted some dying people that assures what I
have called the mobilization of the deepest resources
of life in the coming to light of the Essential, frac-
turing the limitations of the confessionally religious.
This is why it is not important, this witness observes,
for the quality of this moment of grace that the dying
person identifies himself, recognizes himself—however vaguely his or her declining may allow—as one
who confesses this or that religion, this or that confession. It is perhaps only in the face of death that the
religious gets equated with the Essential and that the
barrier between religions, including the nonreligions
(I am thinking, of course, of Buddhism) is transcend-

ed. But because dying is transcultural, it is transconfessional, transreligious in this sense: and this insofar as the Essential breaks through the filter of reading "languages" of reading. This is perhaps the only situation where one can speak of religious experience. Moreover, I am wary of the immediate, the fusional, the intuitive, the mystical. There is one exception, in the grace of a certain dying.

Here, an objection. I am struggling against the make-believe of dying attached to the spectator's gaze for which the suffering person is a dying person; one foresees, one knows with a variable precision that he will soon be dead. It is from this view from the outside on the dying person and the internalized anticipation of this view from the outside on the dying person that I want to deliver myself. So be it. But, someone will say, you appeal to testimony, the testimony of a physician from a palliative care unit. Therefore you are still dependent on an outside point of view in your attempt to separate the dying from the dying person. You do not have any direct access to the lived experience of the dying person in and for itself, if I may put it this way, other than by way of an interpretation of signs gathered by the witness whom you summon to the bar of your argument. A good objection and a good question at the end of the objection. Yes, it is still to a gaze that I am calling on. But it is to[4] another gaze than the one that sees the dying person as dying, as soon to cease living. The gaze that sees the dying person as still living, as calling on the deepest resources of life, as borne by the emergence of the Essential in his experience of still-living, is another gaze. It is the gaze of compassion and not that of the spectator anticipating the already-dead.

Compassion, you say? Yes, but once again it is necessary to understand the suffering-with that the word signifies. It is not a moaning-with, as pity, commiseration, figures of regret, can be; it is a struggling-with, an accompanying—if not a sharing that identifies oneself with the other, which is neither possible nor desirable, a just distance remains the rule for friendship as for justice. Accompanying is perhaps the most adequate word to designate the favorable attitude thanks to which the gaze directed toward a dying person turns toward him, who is struggling for life until death [NOTE IN THE MARGIN: understanding + friendship], and not toward a dying person who will soon be dead. One can speak of sharing despite my reservation concerning the tendency toward fusion or sharing that identifies with the other. But sharing of what? Of the movement of transcendence—immanent transcendence, oh, paradox—of the transcendence innermost to the Essential rending the veils of the codes of confessional religions.

There is certainly a professional aspect to this cultivating of a compassionate, accompanying look: training that masters the motions that tend toward fusion; there is also a deontological aspect concerning behavior (among others between those two extremes so quick to come together: heroic treatment measures and passive, even active euthanasia); but there is also a properly ethical dimension, concerning the capacity to accompany in imagination and in sympathy the still living dying person's struggle, still living until dead.

Could not this other look be that of the physician "trained" to accompany the sick at the end of their lives? Another testimony comes to my mind here, that of Jorge Semprún in *L 'Écriture ou la vie* (1994).[5] It is the testimony of a survivor of the deportation camps (I shall speak later of this other meaning of the terms survive, surviving, linked to another meaning of death than the ones considered here) referring to, at the price of a long agony over writing recounting, the death of Maurice Halbwachs, among the many who died in Buchenwald in 1944. Completely worn out, Maurice Halbwachs was accompanied by Jorge

Semprún. First, in the narration, the most likely, but most indelible signs of giving-receiving, concerning which Peter Kemp says in *Éthique et médicine* that this is the indelible bond of humanity[6]—I was going to say, in anticipation, of the friendship in accompanying a dying person: "Dying, he smiled, looking fraternally at me . . . I took the hand of the dying man who hadn't the strength to open his eyes. In answer I felt only the slightest pressure from his fingers, a light pressure: an almost imperceptible message [giving-receiving already there]."[7] And here the testimony about the rushing in of the Essential: in his eyes: in his eyes, "a gleam of dignity, of vanquished but undiminished humanity. The immortal light of a gaze fixed upon the approach of death, the look of someone who knows where he stands, who's seen everything death has to offer and faces it squarely, weighing the risks and the stakes, freely, with sovereign power" [22]. But it is also necessary to help by a nonmedical, nonconfessional word the still undead dying man: "Then seized with panic, not knowing whether I might call upon some god to accompany Maurice Halbwachs, yet aware of the need for prayer, trying to control my voice, to pitch it properly, I recite a few lines from Baudelaire. It was the only thing I could think of.

O mort, vieux capitaine, il est temps, levons l'ancre . . .

[O death, old captain, it's time, let's weigh anchor . . .]

His eyes brightened slightly, as though with astonishment. I continue to recite. When I reached the line

. . . nos coeurs que tu connais sont remplis de rayons

[our hearts, which you know, are filled with light],

a delicate tremor passed over the lips of Maurice Halbwachs. Dying, he smiled, gazing at me like a brother" (22–33).

This last sentence says it all. M.H. at this instant is alone in dying, but he does not die alone. One will understand this reflection through its contrast to another, equally extreme episode from the same book. A voice is heard chanting the Kaddish. "A voice? More like a bestial moan. The inarticulate groaning of a wounded animal. A bloodcurdling wail of lamentation. . . .—'What is it?' asked Albert, in a low, toneless voice. 'Death,' I told him. 'Who else?' . . . It was death that was humming, no doubt, somewhere amid the heaps of corpses. The life of death, in other words, making itself heard. The agony of death, its shining and mournfully loquacious presence. . . . Albert's face went livid. He strained to hear, and suddenly became frantic, squeezing my arm painfully.—'Yiddish!' he shouted. 'It's speaking Yiddish!' So, death spoke Yiddish" [25, 29, 29–30].

How different from the preceding account: something certainly is said. What is more, it is confessing, confessional: the Kaddish. And a whole history, a whole tradition of suffering is summed up in it. But the dying person, the only one to die, dies alone. It is not another who says the Kaddish. It is not by chance, nor through some literary artifice, that the narrator says that this voice is the voice of death: "It is death humming to itself . . ." Unaccompanied dying renders indiscernible the dying person and death itself, become a character. So the vocabulary drifts: the one dying, death, the dead: is not the Kaddish called the "prayer for the dead"? Prayer said for the dying about themselves? by others with the dying? by death? for the dead? An uneasy hesitation. One can certainly think of the Kaddish said by a dying person about himself: as such, it is a speech-act wherein the whole of Jewish history is condensed ("after all, it was not surprising that death spoke Yiddish," 30). Hence it could be an internalized accompanying word. But this word said about oneself lacks the real compassion of giving-receiving implied by "exteriority" in Levinas's sense.

I come back to the nonmedical quality of the gaze and above all to the gesture of accompanying. It indicates the fusion, in the hermeneutics of the medicine of palliative care, between understanding and friendship. The understanding is directed toward the life coming to an end and its recourse to the essential. The friendship helps not just the person dying but this understanding itself.

3. Jorge Semprún's book, like that of Primo Levi, *Survival in Auschwitz*, forces me, somewhat against my will, to deal with the designation of death itself as an active character as a third make-believe (conceptual) configuration.[8] One will say that what we have is rhetorical make-believe, the same one that engenders prosopopoeia, that rhetorical device that makes the dead appear and speak. But the two preceding configurations already stemmed from a make-believe that I am trying to exorcise through a way of mourning.

At first sight, there is nothing specific, as regards meaning, in what appears to be a fusion of 1) his *death*, upon which rests [around which prowls][9] the question of those still alive: is he still alive, elsewhere, in another fashion? and 2) the dying person, seen from without by those who observe his death without reaching him in his agony.[10] Yes, I would be inclined to believe that personified, active, destructive death enters make-believe at the point where the already dead dead and those dying people who will soon be dead become indistinct.

This is the case with large epidemics—plague, cholera . . .—and what happened in the concentration camps, in that extreme situation where the provisional survivor was surrounded, fenced in, submerged by the indistinct mass of the *dead* and the dying and overcome by the feeling of the great probability of his own death as next, of the imminence of that death. Then he imagines, he perceives himself as already part of that *indistinct mass* of the dead and the dying. I emphasize the effect of mass and indistinction. It is effective only in those limit situations I have spoken of: epidemics, extermination. I want to hold on to the hypothesis that all the living in some circumstances in life, even dreams or the literary imagination, can think of the whole of humanity as already dead and as having to die en masse (Augustine speaking of sin speaks of a *massa perdita*), as a kind of abbreviation, a shortcut. But let's leave to extreme experience what the oneiric can add to, even stand in for. Mass death, that's the theme. It is what above was "speaking Yiddish."

The dread [*hantise*] that confronts Jorge Semprún, once out of Buchenwald, with the alternative: live at the price of forgetting, or remember, write, tell, but be prevented from living, because old-fashioned death would be what was really real and life a dream, an illusion. I need to take seriously this nonrhetorical, lived alternative. But is this death more real than life? To what point is it only a haunting *dread* after the fact, or is it faithful in and through this dread—in the sense of a phantom-like image, *Ghost*—to what had been experienced in that deadly environment, in that contact with the living dead, the dying, mixed together with the already dead dead? Already in the chapter *Kaddish* it is death that hums: "the life of death, in other words, making itself heard" (29). The "smoke from the crematory" as the attestation of death "at work" (29). The dying, death's mouth. To tell, is to tell about death. The essential indistinction: the dying, the "walking corpses" (later signified by Giacometti's *promeneurs* at the Fondation Maeght [45]). The role of *contagion* which from someone living makes someone dying and with the same stroke, someone dead. The contagion that packs together the *massa perdita*. This is the birth of a new sense of "surviving": in the setting of the *massa perdita*. Surviving as *someone who was there* (pogroms, Oradour . . .).[11] The horror of rooms where no one survived.

Survive; to have been saved, the ones saved from the horror. It is with this reference to those who escaped the horror that the figure of Malraux comes to mind, reworking the *Lutte avec l'ange*, for which only the first part ever appeared—*The Walnut Trees of Altenburg*—, remembering the gas attack unleashed by the Germans on the Russian front near the Vistula River in 1916: "Few 'subjects,'" Malraux writes in *Le Miroir des limbes*, "can withstand the threat of death. This one brings into confrontation fraternity, death, that part of mankind which is today seeking to define itself as something far beyond the individual. The spirit of sacrifice is engaged in the most ancient and profound Christian dialogue with Evil: that attack on the Russian front was followed by Verdun, the mustard gas of Flanders, Hitler, the extermination camps . . ." And Malraux concludes (I am still quoting J.S.): "If I return to this event, it is because I seek the crucial region of the soul where absolute Evil and fraternity hang in the balance" (52–53). And this sentence becomes the exergue—one of two—for *Literature or Life*. What is important: to pack together the *massa perdita* of dying and dead it is necessary that the threat of death, directed against you, on purpose, itself should be placed under the sign of absolute Evil, as opposed to fraternity. The pair absolute Evil-fraternity. "The ancient Christian dialogue," says Malraux the agnostic. Must Evil then be named for death to be named and, named, make progress acting against us? Without the mortar of evil, the threat of death would not mix together the dying and the dead, in a horrible epidemic of death. Here lived experience transforms into dread the imagery of Death armed with its scythe. Contagion of the *massa perdita* brought together by a threat, itself summoned up by "absolute Evil," the strong other of fraternity. Thus "a same imperative meditation" (55) can include Kant, Malraux, the narrative of surviving from Auschwitz to Buchenwald, the dying agony of Maurice Halbwachs. For this "same," Malraux's sentence plays the role of connector.

Hence, my question: Would Death be *more real* than life apart from the prosopopoeia of "absolute Evil"?

This poses, it is true, another problem that I shall undoubtedly encounter later on: my conviction that the figures of evil do not form a system, like what one can do in thinking of the good. Auschwitz and the Gulag are *distinct*. The one is not the other: they are incomparable in terms of their *degree* of evil. Is this an objection to an enumeration put together in a manner other than through comparison? by a figuration, why not incarnation (once Jorge Semprún uses the word for the irruptions of death)? However that may be—maybe I shall come back to this—it is not death that is capitalized, but Evil, when the *contagion* is *extermination*, that is, a program of death organized by the Evil One.

Should we then think that, without the limit experiences of *inflicted mass deaths*, Death would never be thought of as an active agent? The great fear. Great fears. See[12] . . . But then, to maintain the primacy of extermination it would have to be that in the popular imagination—our own as well as everybody's—the contagion of great epidemics should be perceived as an exterminating enterprise: first generalization by slippage thanks to which *violent death* becomes a figure of absolute Evil, of hostility (of the Devil? of God? of a vengeful God? perhaps of an Evil One?). Contagion as extermination in the great fears. But this does not suffice: all the dead—those dead of disease, of old age, hence those dead because life has exhausted itself—would have to be *assimilated* to violent death: then extermination could cut into contagion, which itself absorbs banal death into its margins.

No death is banal any more in the shortcut referred to above, where all the deaths get agglutinated into the *massa perdita*. A theology of suffering as punishment has certainly facilitated this fusion-confusion. There is nothing more there than death-*poena* for which one has lost the trace leading back to Extermination. *Every* death exterminates. This is what I take to be the third imaginary figure. It is not a simple fusion of death and the dying person, but catalyzes the *massa perdita* with absolute Evil. *Massa perdita* in a sinister way becomes the *mot juste* in a [PUNITIVE?] theology that takes away the difference entrenched—I would even say by right—in the evil of suffering by the evil of sin through the suffering of pain. In this way, the "old Christian dialogue" so well identified by Malraux the agnostic is doctored into an atrocious theology, both victim and responsible agent of the terror of the make-believe. What we need to do is to return the river to its bed, lead the make-believe back to its place of origin (1). [(1) CORRESPONDS TO THIS NOTE WRITTEN IN THE MARGIN: In this sense this is what J. Semprún does in his book: "The essential part? I believe I know, yes. I think that I'm beginning to understand it. The essential thing is to go beyond the clear facts of this horror to get at the root of radical Evil, *das radikal Böse*" (87). See what I wrote in *Time and Narrative III* about the *tremendum horrendum*, the opposite of the admirable.[13] *The hor-*

rible, the horror of the horrible. "Because the horror itself was not this Evil—not its essence, at least. The horror was only its raiment, its ornament, its ceremonial display. Its semblance, in a word" (87).] Extermination, death inflicted *en masse* by the Evil one. So the capital letter in Death is borrowed from absolute Evil, the Enemy of fraternity.

With this, a difficult road opens: if absolute Evil goes hand in hand with fraternity, mourning must pass through the exorcism of the phantoms generated by absolute Evil starting from the rot of the *massa perdita* where the dying and the cadavers are brought together in their power of pestilential contagion. It is with these phantoms that J. Semprún, *surviving* the death camps, struggles: they are what engender the alternative live and forget or write (recount) and not be able any longer to live.

The phantom: that Death is more real than Life. The horror of death is not Evil, but its appearance.

The phantom: "we are not survivors, but ghosts . . ." (89).

The *camps* revealed the true nature of the horror of death on the basis of a limit situation overlooked by Karl Jaspers: extermination, the work not of death, but of Evil.

My problem is born from this: in what condition

is ordinary death itself contaminated by death at the limit, *horrible* death? And how to struggle against this counterfeit? [NOTE IN THE MARGIN: "What's problematical is not the description of this horror. Not just that, anyway—not even mostly that. What's at stake here is the exploration [in] the human soul of the horror of Evil. . . . We'll need a Dostoyevsky" (127).]

J.S. grafts to the theme of the survivor that of the *unsayable*. True of every death, the event not being there, neither for one who attends nor for the one dying when he "passes." The one event we can never experience individually (89). Lucretius and the Epicureans however are not convincing. Their famous saying is a sophism. Because it is *not* a question of an *experience* but of the *imagination*, always after the fact, always imminent. Too early, too late. "Anguish," "foreboding," "fatal desire" (89). [NOTE IN THE MARGIN: see Landsberg, *L'expérience de la mort*, cited p. 92, p. 168, 20.][14]

J. Semprún [is] the first victim of the make-believe in the *just passed* past, the opposite of imminence. Or rather the recollected imminence in the just passed *counts* as death. The death "I wanted to forget" (108), "the memory of the death" (110). Note: *the* death. Like someone who chants the *Kaddish*. [NOTE

IN THE MARGIN: "a small fragment of the collective memory of our death," *massa perdita*, cited 120.] Do not separate "memory of the death" and "ghost." Only phantoms have a memory of death. The beginning of mourning: "I decided that one had to have *experienced* their death, as we had done, we who *survived* their death (but who do not yet know if we had survived our own), to look upon them with a pure and fraternal eye" [121]. The eye we shall have to turn toward our death, pretentiously assimilated to exterminating death. "These dreadful and fraternal dead" (123). "They needed us to live, quite simply, to live with all our strength in the memory of their death." [THE BOTTOM OF THE PAGE IS PARTLY TORN OFF; THESE WORDS ARE STILL READABLE: memory *heals the make-believe.*]

But memory is nothing apart from recounting. And recounting is nothing without hearing. J.S.'s problem: "How to tell such an unlikely truth, how you foster the imagination of the unimaginable, if not by elaborating, by reworking reality, by putting it into perspective. With a bit of artifice, then!" (124).

Am I getting away here from my own question, my own anxiety, my own make-believe? Not at all; the *detour* is this: if the model of horror is extermination, then the conjuration of ordinary horror passes through the work of memory and the work of mourning (we shall see in part two that they are partly interconnected) accomplished by those who *came back* [sont *revenues*] from death by extermination, from the extraordinary horror, and who as ghosts [*revenants*] have become witnesses, and thereby surpassed—*Aufhebung*—the alternative of literature or life [NOTE IN THE MARGIN: "The essential truth of the experience, cannot be imparted. . . . Or should I say it can be imparted only through literary writing" 125.]

This is what Malraux [HAD] anticipated: "seek"—and find?—the "crucial region of the soul where absolute Evil and fraternity hang in the balance." This search, for me, passes through mourning and mourning has as its intermediary, help, recourse, the work of memory of those who have made life prevail over the "memory of the death." The fraternal assistance of the ghosts become anew the living among us. This is why the *transmission* of their experience is the obligatory road for the therapy of ordinary dying. [NOTE IN THE MARGIN: here the encounter with Claude-Edmonde Magny and her *Lettre sur le pouvoir d'écrire* (136, passim).][15]

What the horror lays bare is the experience that life has of itself and that the Spanish *vivencia* conveys

better than does the French *vécu* and even perhaps
the German *Erlebnis*. The make-believe of Death
whose meaning I'm trying to exegete starting from
extermination up to the *massa perdita* is so anchored
in the *vivencia* that it becomes indiscernible from the
"bare anxiety of living" in its aspect of "chance." The
Luck of tragedy according to Martha Nussbaum.[16]
Why my child? why not me? To survive, like anyone
without merit, hence also without any fault.

[NOTE IN THE MARGIN: How to understand César
Vallejo's verse: "In sum, I possess nothing to express
my life except my death" (144)? Is this *still too close* to
the unexorcized make-believe? Still closer to the horror: "all this life was only a dream, an illusion" (154),
"the deadly knowledge" (156), "to listen endlessly to
the fatal voices of death . . ." (157). The temptation of
forgetting, against "the sorrow of memory" (161).]

Between the *revenant* and life: "I felt myself float-
ing in the future of this memory" (139). To heal memory by telling, without dying of it. This is the "power
of writing," according to Claude-Edmonde Magny.
"That's where I am: I can live only by assuming that
death through writing, but writing literally prohibits
me from living" (163). But: "Did I have the right to
live in forgetfulness? To live, thanks to this oblivion,
at its expense?" (184); *read 208–220*. What then does

33

the passage through Schelling indicate, namely that Evil is not inhuman, once the same fundamental freedom produces the human and the inhuman? Is this, as in Nabert,[17] the unjustifiable beyond the inner limit of norms; here beyond the inner limit of the inhuman? "The frontier of Evil is not that of inhumanity, it is something else altogether" (164). Toward an ethics of Law freed of theodicies?? (ibid.)

The difficulty of writing, of telling by writing: "My stumbling block—but it's not a technical problem, it is a moral one—is that I can't manage to get into the present to talk about the camp, in the present" [166] . . . As though there was a prohibition against presenting it in the present tense . . .

Extend this prohibition to the make-believe of ordinary death. No way of presenting it in the present tense; that is, the moment of dying as a *passing*. Here Wittgenstein: *"Der Tod is kein Ereignis des Lebens. Den Tod erlebt man nicht"* (cited 170). Death is not a lived experience, no *vivencia* of *my* death. [NOTE IN THE MARGIN: Char, *Seuls demeurent*.][18]

→ The meeting point of memory and the work of mourning: "that long mourning process of memory" (186).

This is what helps me in the work of mourning for the make-believe, insofar as its future perfect tense already plunges me in anticipation into the *massa perdita* of dying and dead. Then the way of ghosts [*revenants*], of those who have *returned* [*revenues*] and walked toward life, the way of memory become the way of anticipating the imminence of being engulfed in my turn in the *massa perdita*. So as to hear Baudelaire: "O death, old captain, it's time, let's weigh anchor . . . ," hear it as Halbwachs did.

That the *horror* contaminates *every* death. Claude-Edmonde Magny's citing Keats:

There was a listening fear in her regard
As if calamity had but begun. (193)

All the "do not be afraid" is here in the negative: "the flaw at the heart of all existence" (193).

The alternative in Jorge Semprún's title: only a suicide could sign, voluntarily put an end to this work of "unfinished mourning" (194) that requires "choose between literature or life." (Is this not—it ought to be said more than in passing—another figure of death: *suicide* . . . ??)

Perhaps it was necessary first to have chosen life against writing in order one day to write *and* live? A passage everyone makes, me too, through aphasia? But isn't it from this *state* that I exit in writing these pages? "Mourning of writing" in view of the mourning of memory? For we are not strong. It is necessary to bend a bit, long ahead of time, before facing the storm. For it is also *his* suicide that I have to *accept*. Here J.S.'s question touches me: "Have I really come back?" (196). No anamnesis without "exorcism" (199).

Poorly healed, memory offers only "the chilling yet searing *reflection*" of Evil: "the externalized, radical reality of Evil . . ." (200).

The return of a memory: "This was how—by the return of this memory, of the sorrow of living, I was driven from the mad bliss of oblivion" (219). Say goodbye to forgetting ("to Lorène, unforgettable mistress of oblivion," 220).

225, on the strategy of forgetting.

Until one can say: "*Literature or death*," 231.

It may have been from this that Primo Levi died. For him life *after* will have been "a dream within another dream" (235). . . . Isn't this the road to suicide? That the *massa perdita* is more real than the community of the living. Then *it aspires to join them. Read* the text of Primo Levi quoted, 236: "close at hand, this certainty: nothing is true except the camp, all the rest will have been only a dream, now and forever."[19] Triumph of the future perfect tense: will have been . . . Primo Levi's *Truce*[20] [NOTED IN THE MARGIN: "A dream within another dream, unquestionably. The dream of death, sole reality of life that is itself but a dream," 242. The definition of *no hope* [*inespoir*], to use Gabriel Marcel's appropriate term. Suicide: *signature* on this verdict.]

Why was J. Semprún able to live and write, not Primo Levi?

Because of his strategy of forgetting? → "The courage to confront death through writing" (242). See Abel on courage → Tillich, *The Courage to Be*.[21]

The *temptation* of the suicide [OF] Primo Levi. Regression: "I realized that death was once again in my future, on the horizon" [247]. In effect, in the barely begun mourning of the memory of death, "I lived with the carefree immortality of the revenant." The news of Primo Levi's death: "I become mortal once more" . . . "Death had caught up with Primo Levi." And yet he too had been tempted by the healing of death through writing (quoting p. 248). A book's failure. Primo Levi took the opposite path to J. Semprún, even though at first what was opposite was their *experience* (249). Levi had succeeded there where Semprún had failed. And then the second reversal, which leads to writing: *Nulla era vero all'infuori Lager. Il resto era breve vacanza o inganno dei sensi, sogno* . . . , quoted 251. [NOTE IN THE MARGIN: see Eugen Kogon, *L'Enfer organisé*.][22]

This is what threatens whoever is haunted by the *massa perdita*.

If writing has any chance of working a reconciliation with life, when it sets out to serve the "memory of death," nothing is expected from the narrative technique, from its artifice. Again, memory has to unite the work of memory and the work of mourning. This is what counts for the good use of the memory of death over the course of the exorcism of the make-believe anticipations of this memory that underwrite the elevation of death above the *massa perdita*, to a usurped place that comes down to the "Absolute Evil" named by Malraux. To conquer the dread issuing from the experience of death, of the presence of death in the limit situation of extermination. [IN THE MARGIN: *la vivencia de aquella Antigua muerte*, 281] Dread that can be confronted only by leading it back to "the crucial region of the soul where absolute Evil is opposed to fraternity" (Malraux).

Then, one perhaps discovers that no one has ever experienced death. Wittgenstein talked more correctly about the dread of [BOTTOM OF THE PAGE MISSING],

What is required is the *word* that Heidegger did not say despite the pressing demand from Celan, recorded in his poem "Todtnauberg"[23] which Semprún

quotes p. 289, "the line written *von einer Hoffnung,
heute*."[24] "The hope for a word from the thinker that
comes from the heart." This would be the word that
underwrites, signs the exorcism of the phantom. But
Heidegger's not saying anything is our own, so long as
the phantom of death that kills is not reconnected to
its status as an appearance in regard to absolute Evil,
the other of its other, fraternity. The silence of the
insistence and consistence of Evil, the only "truth" of
the phantom.

Is it because Paul Celan's request—*einer Hoffnung, heute*—was not heard that the poet killed himself, like Primo Levi?

What is difficult and arduous—Spinoza would
have said—the road that Cl. E. Magny indicated to
the future writer: "No one can write unless his heart
is pure, unless he has sufficiently cast off his own per-
sonality . . ." (294). "Writing, if it claims to be more
than a game, or a gamble, is but a long, endless *labor
of ascesis*, a way of casting off by keeping a firm hold
on oneself through recognizing and bringing into
the world the *other* one always is" (295).

There's the rub: the work of memory is the work
of mourning. And both are a word of hope, torn from
what is unspoken. [IN THE MARGIN: Otherwise, César
Allejo's verse remains [293] unanswered:

No mueras, te amo tanto!

Pero el cadáver; ¡ay! siguió muriendo . . .

(but the corpse, alas! continued dying . . .). Verb in the past tense: the future haunted by the past.]

It was fraternity that made him write, the communist prisoner welcoming the newly arrived *Stukkateur* [stucco worker]and not student: "An idea of fraternity still challenging the fatal advance of absolute Evil" (303).[25] Yes, reach the point where the *truth* that expels the phantoms is this: the eternal struggle between fraternity and absolute Evil.

DEATH

Two lines of thought
$\Bigg\langle$ perfect detachment

confidence in God's care

1. Along the first line of thought: dismantling the make-believe of survival pushed to the limit.

a) Carrying to its end the work of mourning: doing so at the expense of any *attachment to self.* "Detachment," according to Meister Eckhart, pushed until renouncing those imaginary projections of self-identity after one's death: the *same* (indifferently *idem* and *ipse*?) in the *same* time, that of one's life before death and that of the survivors who will survive *me*: this is what has to be *lost*. Death is truly the end of life in the time common to me while alive and to those who will survive me. Survival is the others.

b) The ethical dimension of this detachment carried to its end? It is not the courage to renounce

---

Note: This text is from a manuscript with pages numbered 1 to 8, which apparently constitutes the third part announced in the previous manuscript.

imaginary projections—although that "Stoic" component won't count for nothing—but the transfer of the love of life to the *other*. To love the other, my survivor. This "agape" component of renouncing one's own survival completes "detachment" this side of death: it is not just loss, but a gain: liberation for the essential. The great Rhineland mystics not only "negated" themselves, they made themselves available [*disponibles*] for the essential. To the point of being surprisingly active: creating religious orders, teaching, traveling, *founders* (in many senses of the term). This was because they were open to the fundamental through their "detachment" regarding the unessential. So! It is the *openness and being available for the fundamental* that motivates the transfer of the love of life to the other. The relation between openness to the essential, for the fundamental, and the transfer to others who will survive me is reciprocal: openness for the fundamental, freed up by "detachment," *founds* the transfer—the transfer *verifies, attests, tests*, the "test" of detachment in its dimension of generosity.

2. On the second line of thought: the implications of confidence in God. They have to do with the meaning, the intelligibility, the justification of existence.

But think about these implications with no concession to survival in a temporality parallel to the survival of others. Something else than survival. Something other than imaginary projections.

The purely exploratory character of this insight.

a) I have often been touched by an idea that I believe comes from Whitehead: God's memory. God remembers me. Difficult not to put this in the future: God *will* remember me. Risk of making it a hypocritical form of imaginary projection, of "consolation" as a concession to the imaginary—in short, as an *imperfect detachment*. Here appears, for the first time, the question of the *vertical* relationship between time and eternity. The phrase "God remembers me" is said in the eternal present, which is the time of the fundamental, of the essential. However, due to the finitude of human understanding, perfectly expressed as concerns time in the Transcendental Aesthetic of Kant's first *Critique*, I can only "schematize" this eternal present of divine concern. It is this schematism, it seems to me, that gets expressed in *Process Theology* as God's "*becoming*."

It is then in relation to this becoming of God that the *meaning* of an ephemeral existence can in turn be schematized as a "mark" in God. Every existence "makes a difference" in God.[26]

The immense difficulty is to not "represent" this "difference" as survival, in what I am calling a parallel temporality, conferred on the dead by the imagination, as the *encore* temporality of the dead. Properly speaking: the temporality of soul-ghosts.

What can help me to separate the "schematism" of divine memory from imperfect detachment?

Only the idea of *grace*. Confidence in grace. Nothing is owed to me. I expect nothing for myself; I ask for nothing; I have renounced—I try to renounce!—claiming, demanding. I say: God, you will do as you will with me. Maybe nothing at all. I accept no longer being.

Then, a hope other than the desire to continue existing arises.

Can one think of this hope in God's memory using the categories of "salvation"? Only with difficulty: at the price of a radical purification in relation to the Pauline heritage of the redemption of sins. It is a question of an infinitely more radical salvation than the justification of sinners: the justification of existence.

b) I thought I glimpsed something of this justification of existence in Xavier Léon-Dufour's reconstruction of Jesus's attitude in the face of death, short of the Pauline interpretation: the core is [CONSTI-

TUTED] by the paradox repeated six(?) times in the Synoptics: Luke 17:33 *"Those who try to make their life secure will lose it, but those who lose their life will keep it."*

X. Léon-Dufour's commentary p. 39f. *Life and Death in the New Testament: The Teachings of Jesus and Paul.*[27] Cf. "section: life through death." But, already, above p. 22: "Terminology of the Eternal with Time," 27f.: "Jesus used language other than that concerning the after-life and the end of time, and in this he departs from the prophetic tradition," where everything is *future.* According to this tradition, personal survival is thus included in and carried along by the impulse toward the "end times," themselves conceived in a pre-critical way, as a *later* time. The whole rhetoric of a coming judgment exploits this eschatological futurity. Did Jesus think at the limit of this futurity? Traces in the synoptics: the Kingdom of God "is among you" (Luke 17:21). "What had already been suggested in the synoptics became perfectly clear in the fourth gospel. Judgment becomes realized in one's attitude of acceptance or refusal of Jesus as he speaks. It is not only at the end of time that 'the resurrection of the last day' will be granted; already from this very moment the believer 'has passed from death to life'" (John 5:24) [27].

So is that what "has passed from death to life"
means, with no concession to an imaginary survival?

Perhaps the idea of *judgment* needs to be radically demythologized, not only because of its heavy
dependence on *punishment* → the same for salvation-
acquittal, hence for "sin." Or, what amounts to the
same thing, but which is considerably more difficult,
to demythologize "sin"—infraction against the law as
separation from God. So God's *memory* is "pardon"
in something more than a juridical sense of acquittal
or payment, in the sense of a rediscovered proximity.
It is more economical, from the argumentative point
of view, to bypass the category of sin and go straight
to the category of sense/nonsense. There's a chance
then of avoiding the *before/after* death dichotomy.

c) Can the question of meaning be thought of
as a *recapitulation* of existence, in a nonsuccessive
temporality, in a cumulative, thick temporality, com-
pressed into the totalizing instant?

Can one then try to think of *payment* in another
way than as *ransom*, yet still *save the meaning*? John is
undoubtedly the one who has gone furthest in that di-
rection, by offsetting the *before/after* of the prophetic
perspective with the *already here* of the apocalyptic
one (John 5:24–29), according to X. Léon-Dufour.

Can one then preserve something of the futu-

rity of Judgment as a "schematism" of the Eternal?
Yes, maybe, by balancing it with an inverse "schematism" closer to *memory*. But a memory itself distinct
from *recalling a memory*. A memory irreducible to
the pastness of the "no-longer" and in a way exalted
into *preservation of the having been*, the "still there"
of the past "saved" from the *no-longer*, balancing and
matching the "already-there" of the future, *saved*
from the "not-yet."

Continue along the line of the *preservation of the
having-been* as schematization of the "in the past" of
God's *care*, itself schematized as God's memory.

Nothing is lost of what has been. Minimal meaning: nothing could make it that that being had not
existed. But this meaning lacks the *grace* of the sense
of *preserved*.

Not to have existed in vain: "from the point of
view of God" (?) it is true that this make-believe perspective is projected as a protective, sheltering provi-
dence—that is, not a hair of your head falls without
God's having consented to it. This means: everything
makes sense, nothing happens in vain. Schema? inscription in God's memory. [IN THE MARGIN: Conversation with Olivier Abel.]

Perhaps one can add: return of the paradox of
the "first shall be last": in the preservation of the hav-

47

ing-been, those who in appearance "received" and were "given" the least *will receive* more. In this way one preserves something of the idea of a *redress* for injustices in another life. A theme that has motivated many pleas for survival. But think of it in another way than as survival of the same. *A corrective inscription in the Eternal.*

The difficulty: how to conserve something of *lived temporality* (past, present, future), but as a "a schema of eternity"? The temporal dimension of the fundamental. A way of "thinking" in terms of this schematism: balance *memory* (preservation of the having-been) by expectation (what comes, ερχομενος). Yet it is with *expectation* that the danger is greatest of smuggling *survival* back in. Because of this, root *expectation* in the *desire for life* under the sign of perfect detachment. God is the God of the living and not of the dead. What does "and not of the dead" mean? The dead, as the make-believe deceased. The *ghosts* of Sheol, the imaginary fantasy/ ghostly place.

Language can help this difficult schematization: *preserve ≠ conserve.*

d) Can my distinction *ipse/idem* help?

I'm prudent: (maybe a trick of the imaginary) refuge in the *ipse*? Even renouncing *ipseity*?

48

Here "Buddhism" might be of help, insofar as my theme of *attestation* can conceal within itself resistance to "detachment."

I will say today: philosophical defense of the *ipse* for an ethics of responsibility and justice. Renouncing the *ipse* for a preparation for death.

3. Can one think together two lines: on the one side "detachment," pushed to include renouncing the make-believe of survival; on the other, confidence in God's care, "schematized" as God's memory and a *durable* preservation [WRITTEN ABOVE "DURABLE": perennial] of the having been.

Here: the reconstruction by X. Léon-Dufour of Jesus's paradox: "it is through death that existence is definitively assured. This paradox certainly belongs substantially to the authentic sayings of Jesus. Now it is a fact that the gospel tradition has reflected it back six times in exceptional fashion; this shows the importance it enjoys. Behind the various versions of the paradox, scholars think that we can, for the most part, reconstruct the following original saying:

The one who wants to save his *psychē* will lose it

the one who loses his *psychē* will save it" [32].

[NOTE IN THE MARGIN: read X. Léon-Dufour 32f., [WITH REGARD TO] Mk 8:35, Lk 9:24, Lk 17:33, Mt 10:39, Jn 12:25.]

[THE PASSAGE THAT FOLLOWS IS MADE UP OF SHORT NOTES, WRITTEN IN COLUMNS.]

I read in this paradox the *paradoxical* union of perfect detachment:

lose his psychē → renounce survival

want to save his *psychē* → want to survive.

Whoever loses his psychē will save it → preserve in God's care.

Jn 12:25 says something like: Whoever is *attached* to his existence *loses* it and whoever is not attached to his existence in this world will *keep* it in eternal life.

Think about the paradox in verticality, temporality, eternity/safeguard [=] attached to → lose → *keep*.

X. Léon-Dufour proposes p. 32:

"*The one who wants to save his existence will
    lose it
but the one who will lose his existence will
    save it.*"

But this is not the *time of survival*, parallel, for the deceased-phantoms, to the time of the survivors.

How to prevent the future tense of the paradox from smuggling back in the make-believe future of a future life. On the boundary of the "schematism" of eternity and the temporal make-believe . . . On the boundary of hope and any imaginary projection.

This is the whole question of *eschatology* and its imperious imposing of the future of the "last times."

Here is where the fundamental motivation of Jesus is exemplary, inasmuch as the *idea of service* turns the meaning of an immanent death toward the future of the survivors.

It is not the certitude of a literal resurrection that has to be emphasized here—and that can probably be seen [AS] a projection of the Easter faith of the disciples as conveyed by the gospel writers. If that were the case, Jesus did not die like an ordinary human being, even as the most scorned of the condemned. The hymn in Philippians 2 about the self-abasement and *kenosis/necrosis* would be emptied of all meaning. Everything [MUST] be laid bare, and isolated from the Easter context of Jesus's death. Then it is not his *assured* resurrection, but the *transmission from* [*to*] *the other* of his obedience in *service*. One can never overemphasize the correlation in the category of service of "detachment" (regarding oneself) and this "transfer to the other" of the efficacy of detachment, what I above called the positive ethics of detachment. The preaching of the kingdom of God conjoins the negative detachment (renouncing oneself) and the positive force of detachment, of availability for and openness to the essential that governs the transfer of every one of my vital expectations to the *other who is my life after afterlife.*

Jesus knows that his confrontation and his associations lead to death (X. Léon-Dufour takes Mk 2:19–20 to be genuine: "The days will come when the bridegroom is taken away from them, and they will fast on that day.") *Loss* for the friends; their anticipated mourning. Jesus will be gone. A saying [THAT] rings true, without the surcharge of "prophecies edited after the fact" (o.c. 53). A violent death announced, welcomed in *obedience* and *grief.* Jesus could (or had to) apply to himself the kind of tragic fate of the prophets. Whence the "it was necessary." "The Son of Man that he [IS] must suffer much and be despised" (62), "It is necessary that the Son of Man suffer much and be rejected" (Mk 8:31, Lk 17:25).

Violent death. Lk 11:47–51, Mt 23:29–34.

The death of the persecuted Righteous one.

Jesus, says X. Léon-Dufour, is not the subject of the action, but the object of a divine decision, of an "it is necessary" that refers according to all reason to God's plan (63).

Similarly Lk 22:22: "The Son is going as it has been determined."

I do not want to fall into some kind of theological fatalism, some "tragedy," without at least indicat-

ing the counterpart: *plan anticipated and accepted.*
Death situated in a tradition of the violent death of
the prophet.

It is precisely in this core that the detachment
from oneself, in obedience to the mission, and the relation *to the others* get conjoined. Die *for the benefit
of.* This connection, which has been theorized about
in a dubious sacrificial theology in terms of a substituted victim, is at the heart of the Song of the Suffering Servant as *dying for.* To give [IS?] life. The *gift*
transfers [TRANSFORMS?] the detachment for the benefit of the other. Again the theological make-believe
comes back in force as a "redemptive death."

A lovely text from Urs von Balthasar, cited by X.
Léon-Dufour p. 64.[28] Openness to the event. Play
one's role to the end. But a role that has a meaning
[THE END OF THE SENTENCE AT THE BOTTOM OF THE PAGE IS
MISSING]. In this sense one can take up again Mt 20:28
[AND] Mk 10:45. The Son of Man came . . . *to give his
life* as a redemption for the multitude (*lytron anti pol-
lōn*). Whatever may be the case as regards any concession to the ideology of a substituted victim [NOTED
IN THE MARGIN: the sacred and violence]. The *short circuit*: to give his life [FOR THE] multitude suffices, without necessarily passing through a material, corporeal
resurrection. The *Cross-Pentecost* as short circuit.

Abandonment of the one, liberation of many → eucharistic institution. This is my blood poured out for many. Blood ≠ *life*. X. Léon-Dufour is powerful here: "'redemption' is not a sacrificial term" [66]. Sacrificial counterinterpretation of an announced violent death. Frees the field by the pure thought of the gift of life *for*. What is more, even though the *paradox* (above) is repeated five or six times, just one text in Mk and Mt, and none in Lk, makes recourse to the sacrificial language of *redemption*.

The mark of Jesus suffices: "I am among you as one who serves" (Lk 22:27). The opposite of *political domination*: Mk 10:42–45. X. Léon-Dufour is right in daring to say that Mk 10:45: "to give his life in redemption for the multitude" is an addition [68], that the context [is] service.

Service alone, tied to the *gift* of life, destiny and obedience at one time.

For my part I see in this the connection *Cross–Pentecost* to which I shall return in my critique of the narratives about a physical resurrection. Death without an afterlife takes on meaning in the *gift-service* that engenders a community.

The Son of Man is come not to be served but *to serve*. The connection *death–afterlife in the other* is bound up with the *service for . . .* associated with the *gift of life*.

Tie between service and meal. The Last Supper joins dying (oneself) [AND] the service (of the other) in the sharing of the *meal* that joins the man of death to the multitude of survivors reunited in the ecclesia.

It is noteworthy that Jesus himself did not *theorize* this relationship and never says *who* he was. Maybe he did not *know*; he *lived* it in the Eucharistic gesture that joins the imminence of death and its afterlife in the community.

Read X. Léon-Dufour p. 89–92 (emphasizing Hb, on the suffering of Jesus).[29] Jn: passage to glory. But no sacrificial perspective.

FRAG-
MENTS

Time of work,
Time of life

I read on an art book cover: *Watteau (1684–1721)*.

These dates are those of the birth and death of a painter. The parenthesis thereby opened and closed fits tightly around a time of life cut out from historical time. But it does not enclose the time of his work [*oeuvre*], which proceeds from a durability [?] unaware of death.

The proper name Watteau thus designates two distinct referents: the name of the work (one says of a picture: it's a Watteau): an immortal name in the sense that it did not perish along with the painter, and the name of the existing being who once upon a time painted and who died in 1721.

What does it mean for this existing being to die? It means dissociating the immortal from the mortal

---

Note: Several of the fragments were titled "Fragments" (sometimes in capital letters). For three of them we reproduce the numbering P.R. himself gave them, no doubt provisionally: 0(1), 0(2), I.

in his proper name by removing the work accomplished by him.

The two times, that of the work and that of the life, which until then were superimposed, get disjoined: the existing painter deserts the immortal time of the work and withdraws into the mortal time of life (immortal does not mean eternal, but unmarked by the mortality of a living being). [NOTED IN THE MARGIN: The tempo becomes: apprenticeship/debut—the work, fruitful years—decline/the time between the finite work and death.]

This time of dissociation can be experienced as an intermediary time between the immortal time of the work and the mortal time of the living existing being: it is the time of retirement, in the existential sense of *retirement*, the time of *disappearing*.

This is the time I'm in; I still participate in the torments and joys of creation, like a twilight end of season; but I feel in my flesh and my mind the scission between the time of the work and the time of life; I am moving away from the immortal time of the work, and I withdraw into the mortal time of life: this moving away is a kind of dispossession, a laying bare of mortal time in the sadness of having-to-die, or perhaps of the time of the end and of the poverty of the spirit.

[ON ANOTHER SHEET: THIS FRAGMENT:]

The dates of the birth and death of the artist frame the dates of the *production* of each work as an event of life; but these framed dates are simultaneously the moments where the work exempts itself from the time of life and is reinscribed in the immortal—"angelic"—time of the work, the transhistorical time of the reception of the work by other living beings who have their own time.

Fragment I

I.—"A chance transformed into destiny by a continuous choice": my Christianity.

This formula, which has served me elsewhere to eliminate the hypothesis of religious violence as such from my field of inter-religious options, calls for a clarification that will match its ambition. I expect that it will help me to assume, on the hermeneutic plane, the burden of aporias that it bears.

A chance: from birth and more broadly from a cultural heritage. Sometimes I have replied in this way to the objection: "If you were Chinese, there is little chance that you'd be [*sic*] Christian." To be sure, but you are speaking of another me. I cannot choose my ancestors, or my contemporaries. There is, in my origins, a chance element, if I look at things from the outside, and an irreducible situational fact, if I consider them from within. So I am, by birth and heritage. And I accept this. I was born and I was raised in the Christian faith of the Reformed tradition. It is this heritage, confronted repeatedly, at the level of *studying*, by all the adverse or compatible traditions, that I say is transformed into a destiny by a continuous choice. It is this choice that I am summoned to account for, throughout my life, by plausible arguments, that is, ones worthy of being pleaded in a discussion with good-faith protagonists, who are in the same situation as me, incapable of rendering fully rational the roots of their convictions. The title of my discussions with Azouvi and de Launay well reflects this paradox: *Critique and Conviction.*[1] I have also at times proposed a distinction between argumentation and motivation: in the former there is the promise to make sense of the transparent part of my convictions; under the name of motivation I make a place for the opaque part of these convictions; this part is not limited to feelings, emotions, and passions, in short to the irrational side of my convictions, opposed to the rational side of my arguments; it includes everything I place under the heading of heritage, birth, culture. To this continuous choice corresponds the virtue of intellectual honesty, of *Redlichkeit*, which Nietzsche denies Christians. I will not hide the fact that this whole history of arguments, which I am placing under the heading of a "continuous choice," includes moments of individual judgment that, beyond the plausibility of any good-faith argument, do not get beyond a varying degree of probability, on the epistemological plane, the one that Plato, if I am not wrong, placed under the term "right opinion" (*orthē doxa*).

Through this continuous choice, a chance transformed *into a destiny*. By this word destiny I do not indicate any imposition, any unbearable burden, any misfortune, but the very status of a conviction, about which I can say: well, here I stand; this is what I adhere to. (Does not Chouraqui translate the Greek [*pistis*][2] by "adhesion" rather than as "faith"?)[3] The term adhesion is moreover appropriate in the case of Christianity to which . . . I adhere and which includes attachment to a personal figure under which the Infinite, the Most-High, is given to be loved.

It is this destiny whose hermeneutic status I am seeking to express. I will risk characterizing this "here I stand"—another formula for a destiny into which chance gets transformed—by the paradox of a relative absolute. Relative, from the "objective" point of view of the sociology of religions. The kind of Christianity to which I adhere allows itself to be distinguished as one religion among others on the map of "dispersion" and "confusion" after Babel; after Babel does not designate some catastrophe, but rather the mere assertion of the plurality characteristic of all human phenomena.[4] Relativism, if one wishes. I accept this external judgment. However, for me, living it from within, my adhesion is absolute, as noncomparable, not radically chosen, not arbitrarily posited. I cling to inserting the predicate "relative" in the phrase "relative absolute" in order to inscribe into the vow of adhesion the mark of an original chance, raised to the rank of a destiny by a continuous choice. Do I accept speaking of some preference? Yes, in a situation of discussion, confrontation, where the plausible, probabilistic character of the argumentation is made manifest by its incapacity to win out over the adhesion of my challenger. Admission of *public* weakness, of a *strong* adhesion in my heart.

[RICOEUR PUTS A BRACKET AROUND THE MARGIN OF THE FOLLOWING TWO PARAGRAPHS, NUMBERED 2 AND 3, WITH THE SIGN: + farther on.]

2.—My dilemma about the signification for me of the person of Jesus: *quid* of the ideas of satisfaction and substitution in sacrificial christology? Can one eliminate them without remainder? A Christ just a model? *Quid* of the "for"—for us—of the "sacrifice" of the lamb of God?

3.—Support, in the search for a third way, from the hypothesis of a history of God organized elsewhere than in the biblical Scriptures, even of a conversion of the divine, in the manner of the transformation of the *Erinyes* into *Eumenides* in the *Oresteia* of Aeschylus (François Ost's reading in *Raconter la Loi*).[5] God's anger surpassed and conserved in a "fear" of God? [END OF THE BRACKETED LINES.]

2.—I don't want to leave the ground of the hermeneutic status of *adhesion* without having confronted the corollary problem of *reciprocity* in the situation of inter-religious confrontation. The other too can claim the same chance transformed into destiny by a continuous choice. Certainly, from an external point of view, Moses, Jesus, Muhammad, Buddha are to be placed on the same plane in enumerating the founders of religion, and the believers of these multiple forms of obedience have a right to equal consideration. But if one speaks in terms of personal adhesion to one of these communities, the question becomes that of reciprocity and not of comparison; and the aporia arises of the dissymmetry I encounter in the mutuality [I] come to at the end of *The Course of Recognition*.[6] The other will never be an *alter ego*. In Husserlian language, he will never be more than apprehended, reached through an analogizing grasp as regards his intimate act of adhesion at the ground of his conviction. I am speaking in terms of imagination and empathy.

Does this exclude all borrowing, all syncretism? Yes, as an irresponsible and superficial Don Juanism;[7] no, as regards *study* and a transformation in depth of the contents of belief. However, the otherness of the other as other remains irreducible. So there is a political problem in the broad sense of a cohabitation of religious allegiances.

Furthermore, comparison and controversy must not be confused: comparison is looking from the outside; controversy indicates the commitment of the faithful believer to the tradition of his own religion. Each religion is summoned to define itself in distinction and opposition to others: it is in this sense that controversy is integrated into adhesion. And a confession does escape unscathed from this controversy. As Renée Piettre says at the end of an article on the possible relations of Paul's preaching to Epicurean circles, on the occasion of his confrontation with Athenian philosophers at the Areopagus in Athens (in the Acts of the Apostles): "Doctrine arises out of constant interactions and *feeds on what it denies*" (*Diogenes* 205, p. 56).[8] This is how controversy gets inscribed into the history of interpretation and contributes to the formation of traditions of reading and interpretation to which I am the indebted heir.

[THE ADDITIONAL PASSAGE THAT FOLLOWS, ADDED *in fine* TO THIS FRAGMENT, IS INCLUDED IN A BRACKET IN THE MARGIN WITH THE INDICATION + ABOVE; IT HAS TO DO WITH WHAT WAS SAID EARLIER ABOUT ADHESION.]

A propos *adhesion* (*pistis*) and its rootedness in my cultural heritages.

These are rich in textual mediations loaded with history: histories of interpretations generating traditions. My relation to the person and figure of Jesus is thus doubly mediated: by the canonical texts themselves loaded with interpretation and by the traditions of interpretation that are part of the cultural heritage and deep motivation of my convictions. It is in this sense that I recognized myself as "adhering" to the Reformed evangelical tradition. No "immediate" faith.[9]

Fragment 0(1)

I am not a Christian philosopher, as rumor would have it, in a deliberately pejorative, even discriminatory sense. I am, on one side, a philosopher, nothing more, even a philosopher without an absolute,[1] concerned about, devoted to, immersed in philosophical anthropology,[2] whose general theme can be placed under the heading of a fundamental anthropology.[3] And, on the other, a Christian who expresses himself philosophically, as Rembrandt is a painter, nothing more, and a Christian who expresses himself through pictures, and Bach a musician, nothing more, and a Christian who expresses himself through music.

To say "Christian philosopher" is to state a syntagma, a conceptual block; on the other hand, to distinguish the professional philosopher from a Christian doing philosophy is to accept a schizoid situation that has its own dynamic, pain, and small pleasures.

A Christian: someone who professes a primordial adhesion to the life, the words, the death of Jesus.

It is this adhesion that for the working, trained philosopher leads to discerning, to the concern to make sense of, to give the best argument in situations of confrontation and of what I shall later call controversy [IN THE MARGIN: as properly belonging to public expression]. However, this making use of some philosophical competence does not take away the liberty of thought and the autonomy—I would even say the autarky, the self-sufficiency—proper to philosophical investigation and the way it structures its discourse.

Fragment 0(2)

I want [TO SPEAK] without delay about what torments
me in a nagging manner in my relationship of reflec-
tive adhesion to the figure of Jesus the Christ. Is it
simply a matter, if I may put it this way, of following an exceptional model, like one of those prophets
in whom Bergson recognizes the power of a break-
through, invention, a new teaching? Or, at the other
extreme, along the line of sacrificial theologies, of
a death both offered for all people and destined to
satisfy the implacable justice of a God who demands
satisfaction from them for a sin itself worthy of death
and who finds satisfaction in the "substitution" of the
very Son of God the Father who dies in their place?
I have to say that a great part of my argumentative
energy within myself is spent in my rebellion against
this juridicizing of the whole problematic and in a
protest against this sacrificial theory in which I see
the worst use of faith's intelligent understanding of
itself. A revolt that nonetheless has not led me to fall

back upon the use of talk of a model, even one beyond measure. What does the "for us" that is at the very heart of my adhesion to the Reformed version of the Christian tradition signify?

Remaining faithful to a strategy of going slow familiar from my work, I want to seek in extrabiblical traditions encouragement for *another* way of speaking.

But first of all I want to explain myself regarding what I am calling adhesion rather than faith and about its relation to the argumentation that makes me a Christian who expresses himself philosophically.

Controversy

This is the most appropriate concept for making sense both of a situation and an attitude, a practice.

If it is true, as Renée Piettre says, "that a religion exists only by defining itself relative to another one" (p. 135, with regard to Borgeaud),[1] it does so as a *choice* (*hairesis*) "at the expense" of this other, a choice that implies a relative knowledge rather than ignorance and indifference; therefore something like an "observation," and therefore a "comparative history" that opens the way to the "the historian's view from a distance." But then the *adhesion*, by means of which someone faithful to a tradition personally commits himself to the asymmetrical relation that [OF?] "we others" and "all others," strangers in a way, is put in parenthesis. Controversy is a difficult equilibrium between *distanciation* and personal commitment, perhaps what R. Piettre characterizes as a "subjective intellectual position" (135), "able to maintain the historian's distant viewpoint."

I see instead a conflict between the commitment properly belonging to controversy and this view from a distance. Controversy is in this sense distinct from a comparative approach that wants to remain neutral, apart from any religious adhesion.

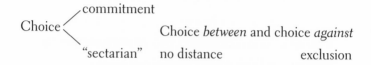

Choice
commitment
"sectarian"   no distance

Choice *between* and choice *against*
exclusion

It is the internalizing of this complex, ambiguous choice that leads to saying: "Doctrine arises out of constant interactions and feeds on what it denies" (Piettre 56).

Interaction as a benefit of controversy vs. [HARM DONE?] to the subject.

The problem finds a sedimentation in the limits of the "theological triangle" [134–35]: Egyptian gods with animal heads, Greek gods with human form, and the noniconicism of the god of the Jews. But all this is drawn from a neutral external point of view, that of the history of religions. It is from this detached point of view that the intersecting glances of one culture on another one along with its corollaries are caught sight of: translation of the one into the language of the other and the comparative evaluation of the one in relation to the other. It is the controversy between

[THE FAITHFUL?] that is thereby separated from its emotional charge linked to the *adhesion* to one or the other [DOCTRINE, WHICH?] gives its note of *struggle* to controversy. One can speak of an oscillation between the struggle and the drama of controversy and the *distanced*—in the sense of not committed—gaze of the historian. If, one more time, one can say that "a religion exists only by defining itself relative to another one," what for myself I have called a "continuous choice" between chance and destiny is not unrelated to that sectarian choice (*hairesis*) which is characterized by the oscillation between committed controversy and comparative distance. This latter is not [THE PAGE ENDS HERE AND NO FOLLOW-UP HAS BEEN FOUND].

The Biblical "Saga" (1)

Reading Finkelstein et al., *The Bible Unearthed* (a [?]).[1]

Beyond the surprise, what remains?

The surprise is great, even for a reader as little attached to the historicity of the characters and the narratives as myself.

There does remain an old ground to which I am going to return: the great antiquity of Abraham, the powerful scene of the crossing of the Reed Sea, the wandering for forty days [*sic*] in the desert under the leadership of Moses, the conquest of Canaan—but above all the genealogical chain of the patriarchs from whom the peoples of the earth descend; the story of Joseph, the glory of David, and the splendor of Solomon's temple, etc.

And now, none of that actually happened, the archeological argument is unanswerable; not a trace of the passage, the occupation of the land, the building.

Nothing historical before the 7th c., before Josiah,

the pseudo-discovery of the Book, Deuteronomy. A small Judah taking over from a more powerful Israel/ Samaria and setting off some fireworks before being swept aside in turn up to the deportation. The return follows, the time of Judaism and the new temple and theography under Persian influence. Here history runs into its bases; textual criticism and archeology go hand in hand.

The surprise therefore of the loss of an *illusion* that itself had been foundational, since Saint Paul, like the Jews of his time, did not doubt the historicity of Moses or his right to appeal beyond him to Abraham, the "father of faith" before and beyond Moses, the father of the law. A great part of the arguments drawn from Scripture rests on the historicity and obsolescence of the narratives of the Torah. Paradox: Jews reproach Christians for having stripped them of their history by metaphorizing it (aside from arguments drawn from "prophecy," which are a more complex problem), whereas that history had been made up and in a sense already metaphorized (which is perhaps what was so specific about the disillusion among Christians, particularly Protestants, who are more exigent about the Old Testament).

The Biblical Saga (2)

What needs to draw our attention, prior to the problem of the writing of the *saga*, running back fictively from the 7th c. toward [THE?] 10th–8th c., is the *function* attached to this invention—to wit, the foundation of a *political* entity that authorizes itself through the history it [HAS] told.

So we have a monarchy not only justified as existing by Yahweh, but by the alleged historicity of its long history. In sum, a *political theology*—a *theological-political* figure. The great age of Abraham functions as the authority for the great age and [THE] great age for the authority. But above all, on the one hand, the genealogy on the ancestral scale allows, by way of procreation and filiation, making sense of the totality of the known populating of the land in terms of a broad, wide-spread *forgotten* kinship; on the other hand, to this exogamic swarm corresponds one that we can speak of as endogamic, since one can consider the Hebrews as one large family that, itself, has lost the trace of itself through the double figure of Israel in the north and Judea in the south. Their genealogical unity justifies, beyond the denial to the Judeans of a right to exist as a distinct legitimate entity, the claim to redistribute all the Hebrews into a single theological-political entity under the aegis of the first Israel, Jacob. The Judeans are henceforth genuine Israelites. A linkage. In this regard the invention—if not of the very characters of David and Solomon—at least of the glory and the splendor of their reign has become a central component of this claim to a hegemonic gathering together contrary to [THE] attested true history.

What is to be said about this essential political construction?

Two very contrasting things.

On the one hand, the admiration reported for the historicity over the *mythopoetical*. What literary genius [?] this political dream has given rise to. What sets this saga apart, in the first place, is that it does not function like the *Iliad* and the *Odyssey* as a fiction parallel to a political history—albeit a moral resource with a high pedagogical value—but precisely as a presumably true history, and in this way founding present history (traces of this genre [?] of saga for me: Saint Genevieve, Roland, Joan of Arc, even Clovis and Charlemagne, better attested to). Therefore, what *mythopolitical power* set in movement, placed at the service of a theological-political application; to found *"historic[ally]"* a theocratic claim.

To here, I gratefully follow my archeological guide. But what this will never explain, especially if it is not combined with textual criticism [SOME WORDS MISSING]; this is why this political theology includes a theological dimension that sets it at the margin of all the political theologies of the ancient Near East— from Egypt to Assyria, Mesopotamia and even Persia (I'll come back to this). What the comparative history of religions (with Borgeaud and Piettre) qualifies as *noniconicity*: a god who is a Name, but with no idol in human form in the Greek manner or with a mixed (animal-human) form.

A theology that sets apart the people that constructs its political theology on this noniconic specificity. From this follows the ethical-theological unfolding unthinkable without this devotion to a Name without an image; no figure, statue, material image. That, the archeological explanation will never explain. On the contrary, it locates itself thanks to this theological anomaly in regard to the comparative perspective. Why Yahweh and not Baal? One does not physically eliminate the idols except to reinforce

[HIM], to recover him. The constantly lost faith, about which the Prophets harangue a stiff-necked people.

The *opaque* core of a political theology for which there is no comparison through the central confession that Deuteronomy proclaims and maybe founds at the same time. *Shema Israel* . . .

Our archeological authors can take pride in belonging to a people that founds Judeo-Christianity and, in a sense, the ethical culture of the West, as important as Greek philosophy and tragedy.

The saga would have remained, like others, pleasant, instructive, through its power to evoke an eventually immense range of experiences, dreams, failures, not only if it had been confined to fiction and if it had [NOT] *founded* a history on the basis of an imaginary history, but if it had based its political theology on another variation of idol worship.

Admiration for the mythopoetical genius of Israel quickly compensates for the first deception of having lost . . . a historical *idol*: the true Abraham, the true Moses; but gets redoubled into a *grateful* recognition of and admiration for the presupposed theology itself.

After Reading Philonenko's Le *"Notre Père"*

It is, he says, an *invocation*, not a *statement*.[1] Does he
mean to say that nothing is said about what God *is*?
That there is no ontology? Certainly, there is nothing
Greek there, as will be [THE CASE] with the Fathers.
But is there not implicitly [SIC], by exclusion, but also
by *possibilization*, something said *about* God.

What is striking about the vocabulary is the
dominance of *acting*. Beyond this, an invocation
is addressed to a God who can do what he does. In
the petitions in "thou" God is asked to *act* so that he
reigns. [IN THE MARGIN: Perhaps a God of the *posse*?
(Richard K.)[2] See other fragment.] The eschatological vision is one of a completeness of *Acting*. The
very structure of the petition is *expectation*, that is,
more than an avowal, more than the optative, namely confidence in the accomplishment of this *Acting*.
Two indications in the vocabulary agree with the
one in the (imperative) grammar, the words *kingdom*
and *will*. The one indicates a sublimated *politics*, the

other a sublimated *psychology*: this is not Hobbes and the problem of human sovereignty, nor Descartes and the will and judgment. *Kingdom* and *will* are on the level of pure *Action*.

The petitions in "us" confirm this:

"Forgive us as we forgive those who sin against us."

We ask to *receive* the acting for us, to the extent of our acting toward others, in the dimension of an offense that is a negative *action* on our part. Two acts are paired: that of God, that of human beings. The *as* (*hōs*) brings about verbally what the unequal symmetry of the two acts carries out in practice.

The last petition, as rewritten by Philonenko:

"And lead us not to the test but deliver us from Evil."

Stages:—action—with a negative note (lead us not)

    —our action put to the *excessive test*

    —the diabolic that engenders the test

Triangulation of the action:

1. Act so that not. Act through a not

2. Human action put to the excessive test. To be tested in one's acting

3. diabolic tempter: enigma of evil that in its anonymity is and is not Someone.

This would be the possibilization that a [OF A?] statement in terms of action. Not Greek. But possibility of a rewriting of the verb being in the manner of Aristotle. Being as *dynamis—energeia*.

Action makes *possible* this rewriting of Greek being. As already in Exodus 3:14–15. See *Thinking Biblically* re "I am what I will be."[3]

FRAGMENT

Jacques Derrida

"I am at war against myself."
Le Monde, August 19, 2004[1]

I take the same starting point: what I do not believe.

If "learning finally how to live" is to learn to die, to take into account accepting absolute mortality without salvation, resurrection, or redemption, I share all the negative here. I too, I do not expect resurrection for myself—as I wrote in *Critique and Conviction.* In the first place, I object to everything make-believe about a [SURVIVAL?] of [?] the survival of [OTHERS?]. I survive but on borrowed time. But no [?], without an [EXEMPTION]. I yield my spirit to God *for the others.* This bond, this transmission has its meaning beyond me and a meaning is concealed there by which God will perhaps join forces with me in a way I cannot imagine; what remains: continue living up to death.

Yes, I am beginning to distance myself from D.

His first look is toward the generation for which he is the last representative. He does not have *contemporaries* to love, and [TO] join his apprenticeship in dying and living. Alone in his terminal illness, in surviving. More an heir than a contemporary. (In this regard, he brings together a group that runs from Lacan to Sarah Kofman, even if he continues to dispute with some of them; but he does bring them together.) [IN THE MARGIN: just one contemporary named: Habermas, but a true vis-à-vis. Brought closer together by September 11.] The confession: "learning to live is always narcissistic," a terrifying admission for fidelity to reading. "To ask me to give up what has formed me, what I have so loved, is to ask me to die." "Yes, Jacques, I say it with you." But I entrust it to my own. My own. I come back to the *for the others* from above. I must say that I cannot link fidelity to deconstruction, even if distinguished from "destructive," but linked to a heartrending, total revolution in language, I see [THERE] a sign of verbal narcissism. That changes the idea of the trace that passes through my own a lot. A thought comes back to me: "the hope that she survives me." All of the religious is there, as a link between my wanting to live and my own. It is true that I do not have the illusion of believing that one has not started to read me. I am quite ordinary and no doubt my works will endure less than will those of Derrida who is really quite extraordinary. But there is the trace of others, to which mine do link up in some way. This is part of the hope that mine will survive. Perhaps that [?], even those who leave no written trace do "make a difference in God"?[2]

Résurrection.

— Niveaux de sens.

entre l'Évangile et
la Structure du
"preuve" liée au
récit

1° niveau nécessaire Exégèse les 4 oppositions controversée / finir par
= Evénement raconté = narratif + miracle → apologie. Fin du miracle
Niveaux ? ? réel Ascension.
Xt ressuscité/signification précède récits. Montée au ciel.

de la mort à la vie → Renversement
promesses accomplies Signes Disciples temps frayeur → Pentecôte
prophétie thèse confesse
Retour "Anaxxx" réunit 1 et 2.

3. Les explic. de victoire de la vie sur mort dans la vie:
une "Renaissance" éspérer "Renaissance" Promesse aussi
"Saison de printemps" Réincarnation Réconciliation
une Saison le printemps Joie le A mien de la vie et Vie éternelle

4. Politique anthropologique Engagement Réconciliation
Niveaux Communion humaine Résurrection notre:
universel ? ≠ 1 printemps Pulsion vitale ≥ pulsions
communication Eros thanatos Tout morts
partage = Structure à l'être au monde? ≠ 1 Elégie
"Éternité"

Structure du temps Exptrrfrer la fête Jugem.
Cela Exptrrfrer que fête s'adresse à communauté
mais aussi aux rites des morts
Travaux d'Heures publics

Résistance de la vie à la mort
Mais ≠ historien Morts le
ce qui était morts ??

5. Eschatologie.
Mort déstruit vaincu
de devenir je des tous pas encore.
Déjà ici bas
agit la mort régne. Anticipation messianique

Resurrection

Level of meaning between the event and
the structure of
being in the
world

1. level   "proof"

apologetics in controversy [?]

= unique recounted event   the miraculous m. → apologetic.[1]

= *narrative* (the Gospel)   End of the miracle at

Ascension.

Ascent to heaven

2. Christ resurrected / signification (*precedes*) narratives

  promises accomplished   *from death to life*

→ *Reversal*

  Messianic *prophecy*   communal signs

Return   Runaway disciple → Pentecost

Come again   compensation

Ascension

     "Announcement" uniting 1 and 2

       glory → Hosanna. Psalm too

3. Experiences of Victory of life over death in life:

     existential level   Success / healing

       historical   2   1

experience: Reconciliation

                                                        3
"Renaissance" = epoch   love of life
"Sacre de printemps"   (joy)   4 and [LIFE   ]
A season: spring

4. Anthropological level
Universal?   Darkness\Light// day night / natural renewal
= communicable
shared   spring   vital impulse ≠ death drive
                   Eros/Thanatos   Freud
      = *structure* of being in the world?   *Desire*
                                              "Being in life"

Structure
of time   ⌠ That explains that the Easter *festival* goes beyond
            | the community
            | but also the rites of worship
            | Crosses through public space
            | ⌠Resistance of life to death
            But   ⟨ victory over death of
                     ⌡ what was dead?

5. Eschatological
    Death of Christ conquered [?]
             The last day   not yet
        messianic expectation
    From here to there:
        death reigns

                                          [EASTER 2005]

90

POSTFACE

The brief account that follows comes from someone who was close to Paul Ricoeur during the last ten years of his life. In it, I try to retrace the context in which the posthumous pages presented in this book were first conceived and written. But let me begin by recalling that Ricoeur granted a special place to those close to him, "those people who count for us and for whom we count." This is clearly indicated in *Memory, History, Forgetting* with regard to birth (132) and also as regards death (359).

The first series of texts—twenty-five pages written in a firm hand—was contained in a folder labeled "Up to death. Mourning and Cheerfulness. P.R." No date is given, but some letters and other documents in the box that contained this folder, along with some things said in our conversations at the time, make me think that this meditation on death was first envisaged following the summer of 1995, and that he began to write about it at the beginning of 1996. Then this material, which he soon stopped working on, was set aside. It ended up in a pile where over the years it was soon buried by other texts, correspondence, and newspaper clippings in one corner of the living room in his home in Châtenay-Malabry. Ricoeur never referred to it again afterward. I only discovered it among other materials several months after his death.

In 1996, Simone Ricoeur, who had shared Paul's life for sixty-three years, was slowly but peacefully dying, as the result of a degenerative disease that saw her grow weaker from day to day, but also still a silent presence in the living room at "Les Murs Blancs." Those who have experienced the passing of those they love will recognize the disarray that such a situation gives birth to and that only increases over time. Ricoeur, unpretentiously, did all he could to make it possible for her to die at home. His meditation on death was written at this time, at her side, in solidarity with her. Visits by Dr. Lucie Hacpille, a specialist in palliative care, gave a rhythm to this period and provided support to them. Still, at the same time the anguish Paul felt was such that, contrary to all this, in order to keep himself alive he added to his meetings, trips, and work commitments.[1] Contradictory imperatives! His meditation on death, "a difficult and late apprenticeship," begun as an ascetic exercise, became a weight far beyond what he could then bear.

This is why, if I am remembering things rightly, he deliberately stopped working on it in April 1997. During these years, I had become a regular visitor to their home. We belonged to the same parish in Robinson, and I hoped that my almost daily visits would help make their burden a little easier to bear, and allow Paul to make his trips while giving Simone every possible attention. She had to be hospitalized at the end of 1997 and died there on January 7, 1998, with Paul and their son Marc at her side.

Eight years passed between "Up to Death. Mourning and Cheerfulness" and his very last writing, which Ricoeur himself titled "Fragments," years during which his "wish to live" was strong and marked by work, writing—the French edition of *Memory, History, Forgetting* was published in September 2000, that of *The Course of Recognition* in January 2004—trips, honors, meetings, and the surprise of the unexpected, of shared friendships that warded off solitude. While editing *Memory, History, Forgetting*, Paul several times confided to me that he was making "great progress" in his reflection on our common "having-to-die."[2] It was at this time that, without wanting or being able to anticipate his own death, we agreed that we would do so together, that I would be the friend who would help him "peacefully to pass away." But, until then, there would be the desire and reaffirmed hope of "living up to death." He told some friends who had gathered to celebrate his ninetieth birthday: "There's the simple happiness of still being alive and, above all, the love of life, shared with those I love, so long as it is given to me to do so. Is not life the first, the inaugural gift?"

However the summer of 2003 (the summer of the great heat wave) interrupted this harmony. A sudden rise in blood pressure caused him to lose his sight in one eye, which caused, as one can imagine, not only difficulty in reading but a loss of equilibrium when it came to walking. This physical degradation even though he still had all his intellectual powers brought about a feeling of depression he tried to struggle against. But it was all the more difficult to bear when, having completed the final editing on his *Course of Recognition*, he no longer was strengthened by the work of writing. In May 2004, a weakening of his heart led to a pulmonary edema whose severity his physicians tried to lessen up to his last night, at home, at "Les Murs Blancs." But age took its toll on his body. Even though having entered what he himself called a "lucid depression," he tried as long as possible to "be there, alive" through reading, following the news, receiving a few friends as visitors, looking forward to conversation, and, once speaking itself became difficult, by listening to music. In June 2004, he decided to continue to write, but now what he called "fragments." These did not make many material demands—some sheets of paper on a clipboard and a pencil accompanied him everywhere; the suppleness and brevity of short texts where he could present his reactions to the reader, add to his reflections on the themes dear to him and to those commitments that had marked his life: "to become capable of dying" was his present concern.

Starting in September his sense of getting closer to death grew. "People see me as looking better than I feel" was something he said often then. Then, "I know it is coming, I am in the process of disappearing"—and a few days before his death: "I have entered a unique time . . ." This was a difficult period for him: to the humiliation of finding himself so weak, dependent, "suffering" and not "acting," more and more dominated by sleep and an extreme fatigue was added the anxiety that he tried to name without being able to evade it: "Of course there is an anxiety about nothingness . . ." I retain the memory of his painful struggle with himself, despondency, sometimes fear, and despite all our efforts, especially at night, the sense of solitude of someone on the way out, but always repeating beyond such torments his will to "honor life" until death. A note sent several weeks before his dying to a slightly younger friend, herself having reached the evening of life, seems to me to contain something of the tension he was feeling then, if one is attentive to the breaks created by its punctuation:

> Dear Marie,
> At the hour of decline the
> word resurrection arises. Beyond
> every miraculous episode. From the depths of life,
> a power suddenly appears, which says that being is
> being against death.
> Believe this with me.
>   your friend,
>   Paul R.

The first of the fragments from this final year dates from June 2004. "Time of work, time of life" was written almost as a note to the others. Then, at the end of June, fragment I: "A chance transformed into destiny by a continuous choice," followed by two more: fragment o(1): "I am not a Christian philosopher . . ." and fragment o(2): "I want [TO SPEAK] without delay . . . ," then by "Controversy." Over the course of July, August, and September he wrote "The

Biblical 'Saga,'" "After reading Philonenko's *Le 'Notre Père'*" and "Jacques Derrida." The last fragment, "Resurrection—levels of meaning," which was written down as a rough draft, dates from around Easter 2005. It is more an outline than a text, and Ricoeur's handwriting, which is impossible to read at some points, had by then deteriorated considerably.

Some words we found scratched on the back of one sheet at the time of our beginning to edit these fragments may serve to justify our decision to publish them: "time of writing separated by death from the time of publication → 'posthumous.'"

Catherine Goldenstein

NOTES

1. Ricoeur left the many books used in his work and the papers relating to it to what is now the Fonds Ricoeur, housed in the library of the Protestant Faculty of Theology in Paris. The website for this collection can be found at www.fondsricoeur.fr.

2. Paul Ricoeur, *Memory, History, Forgetting,* trans. Kathleen Blamey and David Pellauer (Chicago: University of Chicago Press, 2004).

3. Regarding this change of sign applied to that of a "limit" and to a "conversion to this side," see what Ricoeur said in "Pierre Thévenaz, un philosophe protestant," in *Lectures 3: Aux frontières de la philosophie* (Paris: Seuil, 1994), 245–59; see also his "Freedom in the Light of Hope," in *The Conflict of Interpretations* (Evanston: Northwestern University Press, 1974), 402–24.

4. What Ricoeur criticized in Heidegger was the hierarchy he established between a heroic authenticity of anxiety that continually faced up to its death and the banality of an inauthenticity that tried to flee death. Ricoeur instead called on Spinoza, for whom wisdom was a meditation not on death

but on life and on living "until . . ." See, for example, *Memory, History, Forgetting*, 357. There Ricoeur also says that "Levinas is clear and firm regarding the before, which can only be a being-against-death and not a being-toward-death" (361).

5. See the chapter titled "The Way of Consent." in Paul Ricoeur, *Freedom and Nature: The Voluntary and the Involuntary*, trans. Erazim V. Kohák (Evanston: Northwestern University Press, 1966), 444–81, which takes up in turn Stoicism (or imperfect consent) and Orphism (or hyperbolic consent), to end with consent based on hope.

6. Ricoeur proposes here a tentative passage between texts drawn from Jorge Semprún and Primo Levi.

7. "Evil: A Challenge to Philosophy and Theology," in *Figuring the Sacred*, ed. Mark I. Wallace, trans. David Pellauer (Minneapolis: Fortress Press, 1995), 249–61; *The Course of Recognition*, trans. David Pellauer (Cambridge, MA: Harvard University Press, 2005).

8. Paul Ricoeur, *Critique and Conviction: Conversations with François Azouvi and Marc de Launay*, trans. Kathleen Blamey (New York: Columbia University Press, 1998), 158. "Admissions without being confessions" was what he inscribed in the copy of this work he gave me.

9. Although he continued to say that he took seriously all the traditions transmitted by the different church traditions, even when he felt more or less removed from them, as though each of them were one part of an irreducible experience.

10. I subsequently published these thoughts in "Élegie à la resurrection," *Études*, no. 392 (April 2000): 497–500.

11. Which undoubtedly can be dated to 1996 or thereabouts.

12. *Critique and Conviction*, 145.

13. Renée Piettre, cited in these fragments, has shown how *pistis* was in some ways invented by the Epicureans to make manifest how radical was the commitment and conversion presupposed by adhering to the theses of the Garden: "Épicure, dieu et image de dieu: une autarcie extatique," *Revue de l'Histoire des Religions* 119 (1999): 5–30.

14. This was the topic of an intense conversation Ricoeur had toward the end of his life with Hans-Christoph Askani, who was then professor in the Protestant Faculty in Paris, and who lived near Ricoeur. Looking for a third way, Ricoeur was particularly interested in the conversion of the tragic god of the furies, the Erinyes, into the god of the Eumenides in Sophocles' *Oedipus at Colonus*.

15. "When have we seen thee hungry, and fed thee? . . . As long as you did it to one of the least of my brethren, you did it to me" (Matthew 25:37–40), cited in Paul Ricoeur, "The Socius and the Neighbor," in *History and Truth*, trans. Charles A. Kelbley (Evanston: Northwestern University Press, 1965), 100.

16. A way of thinking of *ipseity* itself not as a way of saving oneself but as the expression of a demand for responsibility toward and justice for others.

UP TO DEATH: MOURNING AND CHEERFULNESS

1. Paul Ricoeur, *Freedom and Nature: The Voluntary and the Involuntary*, trans. Erzaim V. Kohák (Evanston: Northwestern University Press, 1966), 447–48.

2. Probably a reference to Karl Barth's famous and influential commentary on Romans. For an English translation see, *The Epistle to the Romans*, trans. Edwyn C. Hoskyns (New York: Oxford University Press, 1933). —Trans.

3. Northrop Frye, *The Great Code: The Bible and Literature* (New York: Harcourt Brace Jovanovich, 1982).

4. The text has "from an." A few words earlier Ricoeur changed the text "from a gaze" to "to a gaze," but he undoubtedly forgot to change it in this sentence.

5. Jorge Semprún, *Literature or Life*, trans. Linda Coverdale (New York: Viking, 1997).

6. Peter Kemp, *Éthique et médicine* (Paris: Tierce, 1987).

7. Semprún, *Literature or Life*, 22. The words in brackets are Ricoeur's.

8. Primo Levi, *Survival in Auschwitz: The Nazi Assault on Humanity*, trans. Stuart Woolf (New York: Collier Books, 1993).

9. Ricoeur writes this second form under the first one, without crossing out the first one.

10. Added above this text: "another kind of surviving = attending."

11. The German Führer Regiment of the Waffen-SS Panzer Division Das Reich burned the French village of Oradour-sur-Glane on June 10, 1944, killing 642 men, women, and children. —Trans.

12. No reference given. Perhaps an allusion to the work of Jean Delumeau on fear: *Sin and Fear: The Emergence of a Western Guilt Culture, 13th–18th Centuries*, trans. Eric Nicholson (New York: St. Martin's, 1990).

13. Paul Ricoeur, *Time and Narrative*, vol. 3, trans. Kath-

leen Blamey and David Pellauer (Chicago: University of Chicago Press, 1988), 187.

14. Paul Landsberg, *Essai sur l'expérience de la mort* (Paris: Seuil, 1951), reprinted in 1993. Ricoeur had written a review of this book for *Esprit* in 1951, reprinted in his *Lectures 2: La contrée des philosophes* (Paris: Seuil, 1992), 191–94.

15. Claude-Edmonde Magny, *Lettre sur le pouvoir d'écrire* (Paris: Seghers, 1947), is cited in Semprún's text.

16. Martha Nussbaum, *The Fragility of Goodness: Luck and Ethics in Greek Tragedy* (New York: Cambridge University Press, 1986).

17. Jean Nabert, *Elements for an Ethic*, Preface by Paul Ricoeur, trans. William J. Petrek (Evanston: Northwestern University Press, 1969).

18. René Char, *Seuls demeurent*, a poem from 1945, published in the collection of Char's poems, *Fureur et mystère* (Paris: Gallimard, 1948).

19. Translation altered to convey the French verb form.

20. The Italian title of Levi's book was *La tregua*; translated as *The Reawakening*, trans. Stuart Woolf (New York: Collier, 1986).

21. Ricoeur refers to an unpublished book on discouragement by Olivier Abel, and to Paul Tillich, *The Courage to Be* (New Haven: Yale University Press, 1952).

22. Eugen Kogon, *The Theory and Practice of Hell: The German Concentration Camps and the System behind Them*, trans. Heinz Norden (London: Secker and Warburg, 1950; New York: Berkeley Books, 1998).

23. Todtnauberg is the name of the village in the Black Forest where Heidegger lived.

24. In hope, today.

25. If Semprún had been listed as a student (*Student*), he says that most likely he would have been immediately sent to the gas chamber. —Trans.

26. The phrase "makes a difference" is in English in the French manuscript.

27. Xavier Léon-Dufour, *Life and Death in the New Testament: The Teachings of Jesus and Paul*, trans. Terrence Pendergast (San Francisco: Harper and Row, 1986).

28. "To deprive Jesus of this opportunity and make him advance toward a goal which he already knows and which is distinct only in time, would mean stripping him of his dignity as a man." Hans Urs von Balthasar, *La foi du Christ* (Paris: Aubier, 1969), 181.

29. The Book of Hebrews.

FRAGMENT I

1. Paul Ricoeur, *Critique and Conviction: Conversations with François Azouvi and Marc de Launay*, trans. Kathleen Blamey (New York: Columbia University Press, 1998).

2. The word is not given here, but is cited below.

3. André Chouraqui's translation of the Bible into French is well known as an attempt to convey the force and originality of the Hebrew and of biblical teaching, one that has been both admired and criticized.

4. See Paul Ricoeur, "The Paradigm of Translation," in *Reflections on the Just*, trans. David Pellauer (Chicago: University of Chicago Press, 2007), 106–20. Another translation of this

essay appears in Paul Ricoeur, *On Translation*, trans. Eileen Brennan (New York: Routledge, 2006), 11–29. — Trans.

5. François Ost, *Raconter la loi: Aux sources de l'imagination juridique* (Paris: Odile Jacob, 2004).

6. Paul Ricoeur, *The Course of Recognition*, trans. David Pellauer (Cambridge, MA: Harvard University Press, 2005), 150–61.

7. Ricoeur had leveled this charge against Karl Jaspers's philosophy of religion in "The Relation of Jaspers' Philosophy to Religion," in Paul A. Schlipp, ed., *The Philosophy of Karl Jaspers* (New York: Tutor, 1957), 611–42. — Trans.

8. Renée Piettre, "Paul and the Athens Epicureans: Between Polytheisms, Atheisms, and Monotheisms," *Diogenes* 52, no. 205 (January–March 2004): 47–60. This issue on pluralism and cultural diversity was edited by Piettre, who is the author of the introduction (5–11) and the article cited. She also reviews (134–39) Paul Borgeaud, *Aux origines de l'histoire des religions* (Paris: Seuil, 2004).

9. "No immediate faith" is crossed out, then repeated.

FRAGMENT O(1)

1. Jean Greisch [Ricoeur's own note]. See Greisch, "La métamorphose herméneutique de la philosophie de la religion," in Jean Greisch and Richard Kearney, eds., *Paul Ricoeur: Les métamorphoses de la raison herméneutique* (Paris: Cerf, 1991), 311–34; and Greisch, *Paul Ricoeur: L'itinérance du sens* (Paris: Jérôme Million, 2001). — Trans.

2. The three adjectives are written above one another in the manuscript.

3. To use an expression of the Swiss philosopher Pierre Thévenaz, another Protestant, like me [Ricoeur's own note].

CONTROVERSY

1. Renée Piettre, review of Philippe Borgeaud, *Aux origins de l'histoire des religions*, *Diogenes* 52, no. 205 (January–March 2004): 134–39.

THE BIBLICAL "SAGA" (1)

1. Israël Finkelstein and Neil Asher Silberman, *The Bible Unearthed: Archeology's New Vision of Ancient Israel and the Origin of Its Sacred Texts* (New York: Free Press, 2001). The French translation of this book, *La Bible dévoilée: Les nouvelles révélations de l'archéologie*, trans. Patrice Ghirardi (Paris: Bayard, 2002), which was a best seller, presents the "best attested historical knowledge" on the basis of archeology about the Bible dating from the seventh, even the sixth century, BC. Nothing for certain is known not only about Moses (fourteenth century BC), but also about the first kings of Israel—in particular about David and Solomon (tenth century BC)—and what can be known turns out to be based on very fragile evidence.

AFTER READING PHILONENKO'S *Le "Notre Père"*

1. Marc Philonenko, *Le "Notre Père": De la prière de Jésus à la prière des disciples* (Paris: Gallimard, 2001).

2. See Richard Kearney, "Enabling God," in John Pan-teleimon Manoussakis, ed., *After God: Richard Kearney and the Religious Turn in Philosophy* (Bronx: Fordham University Press, 2006), 39–54; and Richard Kearney, *The God Who May Be: A Religious Hermeneutics* (Bloomington: Indiana University Press, 2001).

3. Paul Ricoeur, "From Interpretation to Translation," in André LaCocque and Paul Ricoeur, *Thinking Biblically: Exegetical and Hermeneutical Studies*, trans. David Pellauer (Chicago: University of Chicago Press, 1998), 331–61.

JACQUES DERRIDA

1. This article is based on an interview with Derrida, who died on October 9, 2004.

2. "Make a difference in God" is in English in the French manuscript.

RESURRECTION

1. The phrase "miraculous man" refers to the risen Jesus in the period between Easter and Pentecost.—Trans.

POSTFACE

1. In a list in his pocket calendar for 1996–1997 I found this summary of his trips for this period, listed almost as if to verify that everything was still normal.

Ulm

March: Saint Petersburg/Moscow

15 April: Naples

28 May: Copenhagen

October: Rome Venice

Namur

July: Dublin

30 Sept. 4 Oct.: Oslo

12–15 Oct.: Freiberg

26–29 Oct.: Sophia

6 Nov. Avignon TGV [*train à grande vitesse*, the French high-speed railway]

2. Frédéric Worms has recognized and presented these advances in his essay "Vivant jusqu'à la mort . . . et non pas pour la mort," in the memorial issue of *Esprit* dedicated to Ricoeur, no. 323 (March–April 2006): 304–11.